श्रीशुक्लयजुर्वेदीय
रुद्राष्टाध्यायी

Śrī Śukla Yajurvedīya
Rudrāṣṭādhyāyī

By
स्वामी सत्यानन्द सरस्वती
Swami Satyananda Saraswati
and
स्वामी विट्ठलानन्द सरस्वती
Swami Vittalananda Saraswati

Published By
Devi Mandir Publications

रुद्राष्टाध्यायी **Rudrāṣṭādhyāyī**,

by Devi Mandir Publications
5950 Highway 128
Napa, CA 94558 USA
Communications: Phone and Fax 1-707-966-2802
E-Mail swamiji@shreemaa.org
Please visit us on the World Wide Web at
http://www.shreemaa.org/

ISBN 1-877795-53-4
Library of Congress Control Number: 2001127224

रुद्राष्टाध्यायी **Rudrāṣṭādhyāyī**,
Swami Satyananda Saraswati
1. Hindu Religion. 2. Worship. 3. Spirituality.
4. Philosophy. I. Saraswati, Swami Satyananda;
Saraswati, Swami Vittalananda

Contents

Introduction	1
Chapter One	31
Chapter Two	36
Chapter Three	44
Chapter Four	51
Chapter Five (Nāmakam)	58
Chapter Six	91
Chapter Seven	95
Chapter Eight (Camakam)	100
Chapter Nine (Śāntyadhyāyaḥ)	118
Ārati	132
Praṇām	137

May Lord Shiva bless us all.

Introduction

The Rudrāṣṭādhyāyī, or Eight Chapters in Praise of Rudra, is one of the most acclaimed and celebrated hymns to Śiva in the world. It is chanted continually in all Śiva temples and especially in all the *jyotir lingams*, the special places of pilgrimage for Lord Śiva in India, where Śiva has bestowed his eternal light as a blessing to every devotee who comes to pray with devotion.

The Rudrāṣṭādhyāyī celebrates Śiva, the Consciousness of Infinite Goodness, in his form as the Reliever of Sufferings. Rudra comes from the Saṃskṛta, *asru trayate*, he who takes away the tears. Rudra is the form of Śiva who takes away our tears, and puts an end to all suffering.

The Rudrāṣṭādhyāyī emanates from the Śukla Yajur Veda. The Vedas are the oldest expressions of spiritual wisdom known to mankind. According to religious scholars, the Vedas were one with God at the origin of creation. According to historians, they are considered to be between 5,000 and 20,000 years old. The Vedas were originally perceived by enlightened beings called *Ṛṣis*, seers of the eternal harmony which is one with God. These Ṛṣis intuitively understood the wisdom of the Vedas, that Infinite Consciousness joined with the totality of Nature to manifest every object and relationship in existence. By uniting their consciousness with the Supreme Consciousness, the Ṛṣis became aware of this imperishable wisdom which expresses the harmony of all existence in universal consciousness.

Another name for a Ṛṣi is a Kavi, or inspired poet. The Ṛṣis expressed the wisdom of this universal harmony through inspired poetry. These poems were recited by the Ṛṣis and memorized by their disciples in a process called *śruti*, that which is known through hearing.

The hymns and poems were passed down from generation to generation through the disciplic succession until one generation of disciples said, "This is too much for us. We cannot memorize all of this material, no matter how much wisdom it contains." The Vedas were then divided into four parts: the Rig Veda - the wisdom of hymns, the Yajur Veda - the wisdom of the sacrifice of egotistical attachment, the Sāma Veda - the wisdom of song, and the Atharva Veda - the wisdom of how to apply spiritual knowledge to our daily lives.

Because this quantity of knowledge was still so voluminous, the four Vedas were further divided into four sections: Saṃhitā, or hymns; Araṅyaka, stories about the lives of the ṛṣis; Brahmāṇas, texts that explain to the priests how to conduct the ceremonies, and Upaniṣads, the philosophy of maintaining unity consciousness.

The Rudrāṣṭādhyāyī comes from the Śukla section of the Yajur Veda. The Śukla section, or the bright illuminated portion, are hymns that inspire humanity to express unity consciousness in all actions they perform.

The Eight Chapters in Praise of Rudra from the Śukla Yajur Veda actually contains nine chapters. The first chapter is a prayer to receive the *saṅkalpa*, or determination and focus of mind of Śiva. The second chapter praises Śiva in His omnipresence. The third chapter is a blessing for the spiritual warrior within us, to prevail in the battle and defeat our own enemies. In the fourth chapter we praise Śiva as the light of wisdom. In the fifth chapter we bow to Śiva in all His forms. In the sixth chapter we ask for His blessings. In the seventh chapter we make offerings to His various manifestations. In the eighth chapter we recite many of His divine characteristics that are within us. In the ninth chapter we ask for peace and offer peace to all existence.

Chapter Five has become especially famous as the *Nāmakam*, because the verses contain special names of Śiva to which we bow (Nāmaṇa kara) in devotion and offer our oblations. Chapter Eight is known as the *Camakam*, because it contains a list of characteristics and qualities that are within us, and after each quality *ca* is inserted, meaning *and*. Therefore it is called *Camakam*. The Eight Chapters in Praise of Rudra actually contain nine, and the ninth chapter is known as the *Śāntyadhyāyaḥ*, the chapter that conveys the blessings of peace.

The Rudrāṣṭādhyāyī has been chanted for thousands of years by millions of people. The feeling and wisdom of these beautiful hymns of praise have been transmitted from generation to generation in the oral tradition of the Guru-disciple relationship. Those who chant the Rudrāṣṭādhyāyī can feel the vibrations of these many generations of sincere worshippers and can receive this transmission themselves.

These Vedic poems convey the spiritual emotion, or *bhāva*, of the passionate love and worship of Śiva. These hymns help to take away our suffering and grant us peace. They are filled with inspiration, and the tones of their chanting conduct our vibrations to radiant purity. As we continue to sing these hymns and invoke Śiva, we experience more and more love for God. Śiva comes to us and give us His *darśana*, the blessed vision of His divine presence.

Shree Maa reminds us that these poems teach us that we are one with everything and everything is within us. Therefore we must respect all beings and respect our own actions. If we unite with God by giving up selfish attachments, and see the love for God in every action we perform, we will discover that the divinity we are seeking is within us, as well as all around us. We become divine beings in a divine paradise, and occasionally take little trips to visit the world of human interaction.

Shree Maa joins me in offering all the blessings of Lord Śiva.

Swami Satyananda Saraswati
Devi Mandir, 2002

देवता प्रणाम्
devatā praṇām

श्रीमन्महागणाधिपतये नमः

śrīmanmahāgaṇādhipataye namaḥ
We bow to the Respected Great Lord of Wisdom.

लक्ष्मीनारायणाभ्यां नमः

lakṣmīnārāyaṇābhyāṃ namaḥ
We bow to Lakṣmī and Nārāyaṇa, the Goal of all Existence and the Perceiver of all.

उमामहेश्वराभ्यां नमः

umāmaheśvarābhyāṃ namaḥ
We bow to Umā and Maheśvara, She who protects existence, and the Great Consciousness or Seer of all.

वाणीहिरण्यगर्भाभ्यां नमः

vāṇīhiraṇyagarbhābhyāṃ namaḥ
We bow to Vāṇī and Hiraṇyagarbha, Sarasvatī and Brahmā, who create the cosmic existence.

शचीपुरन्दराभ्यां नमः

śacīpurandarābhyāṃ namaḥ
We bow to Śacī and Purandara, Indra and his wife, who preside over all that is divine.

मातापितृभ्यां नमः

mātāpitṛbhyāṃ namaḥ
We bow to the Mothers and Fathers.

इष्टदेवताभ्यो नमः

iṣṭadevatābhyo namaḥ
We bow to the chosen deity of worship.

कुलदेवताभ्यो नमः

kuladevatābhyo namaḥ
We bow to the family deity of worship.

ग्रामदेवताभ्यो नमः

grāmadevatābhyo namaḥ
We bow to the village deity of worship.

वास्तुदेवताभ्यो नमः

vāstudevatābhyo namaḥ
We bow to the particular household deity of worship.

स्थानदेवताभ्यो नमः

sthānadevatābhyo namaḥ
We bow to the established deity of worship.

सर्वेभ्यो देवेभ्यो नमः

sarvebhyo devebhyo namaḥ
We bow to all the Gods.

सर्वेभ्यो ब्राह्मणेभ्यो नमः

sarvebhyo brāhmaṇebhyo namaḥ
We bow to all the Knowers of divinity.

शिव ध्यानम्
śiva dhyānam

ॐ सदा शिवाय विद्महे सहश्राक्षाय धीमहे ।

तन्नो शम्भो प्रचोदयात् ॥

oṃ sadā śivāya vidmahe sahaśrākṣāya dhīmahe
tanno śambho pracodayāt

oṃ We meditate upon the Perfect, Full, Complete, Always Continuing, Consciousness of Infinite Goodness; contemplate He Whose Thousand Eyes see everywhere. May that Giver of Bliss grant us increase.

ॐ सद्योजातं प्रपद्यामि सद्योजातायवै नमो नमः ।

भवे भवे नाति भवे भवस्वमांभवोद्भवाय नमः ॥

oṃ sadyojātaṃ prapadyāmi
sadyojātāyavai namo namaḥ
bhave bhave nāti bhave
bhavasvamāṃ bhavodbhavāya namaḥ

oṃ I extol the Birth of Truth as Pure Existence. Again and again I bow down to the Birth of Truth as Pure Existence. In being after being, beyond all being, who Himself is all Being, from whom came all being, to That Existence I bow.

वामदेवाय नमो ज्येष्ठाय नमः श्रेष्ठाय नमो रुद्राय नमः ।

कालाय नमः कलविकरणाय नमो बलविकरणाय नमो

बलाय नमो बलप्रमत्तनाय नमः । सर्वभूतदमनाय

नमोमनोन्मनाय नमः ॥

vāmadevāya namo jyeṣṭhāya namaḥ śreṣṭhāya namo rudrāya namaḥ kālāya namaḥ kalavikaraṇāya namo balavikaraṇāya namo balāya namo balapramattanāya namaḥ sarvabhūtadamanāya namomanonmanāya namaḥ

I bow to the Beautiful God who is Beloved. I bow to the Pleasant One, to the Ultimate One; I bow to the Reliever of Sufferings. I bow to Time, I bow to the Cause of the Illumination of Darkness, I bow to the Source of Strength, I bow to the Progenitor of Strength. I bow to the Fashioner of all the elements, I bow to the Mind of all minds.

अघोरेभ्योत्तघोरेभ्योघोरघेरतरेभ्यः ।

सर्वेभ्यःसर्वशर्वेभ्यो नमस्तेऽस्तुरुद्ररूपेभ्यः ॥

aghorebhyottaghorebhyoghoragheratarebhyaḥ sarvebhyaḥsarvaśarvebhyo namaste-sturudrarūpebhyaḥ

I bow to He who is Free From Fear, who instills the fear of evil, who saves the righteous from fear; who is within all, the all of everything, may we give our respect to He who is the form of the Reliever of Sufferings.

ॐ तत् पुरुषाय विद्महे महादेवाय धीमहि ।

तन्नो रुद्रः प्रचोदयात् ॥

oṃ tat puruṣāya vidmahe mahādevāya dhīmahi tanno rudraḥ pracodayāt

oṃ We meditate upon That Universal Consciousness, contemplate the Great God. May that Reliever of Sufferings grant us increase.

ईशानः सर्वविद्यानमीश्वरः सर्वभूतानाम् ।

ब्रह्माधिपतिर्ब्रह्मणोधिपतिर्ब्रह्माशिवोमेऽस्तुसदाशिवोम् ॥

īśānaḥ sarvavidyānamīśvaraḥ sarvabhūtānām brahmādhipatirbrahmaṇodhipatirbrahmāśivome-stusadāśivom
The Seer of All, who is all Knowledge, the Lord of the Universe, who is all existence; before the Creative Consciousness, before the knowers of Consciousness, existing in eternal delight as the Consciousness of Infinite Goodness.

ॐ अग्निर्ज्योतिर्ज्योतिरग्निः स्वाहा ।

सूर्यो ज्योतिर्ज्योतिः सूर्यः स्वाहा ।

अग्निर्वर्चो ज्योतिर्वर्चः स्वाहा ।

सूर्यो वर्चो ज्योतिर्वर्चः स्वाहा ।

ज्योतिः सूर्यः सूर्यो ज्योतिः स्वाहा ॥

oṃ agnir jyotir jyotir agniḥ svāhā
sūryo jyotir jyotiḥ sūryaḥ svāhā
agnir varco jyotir varcaḥ svāhā
sūryo varco jyotir varcaḥ svāhā
jyotiḥ sūryaḥ sūryo jyotiḥ svāhā
oṃ The Divine Fire is the Light, and the Light is the Divine Fire; I am One with God! The Light of Wisdom is the Light, and the Light is the Light of Wisdom; I am One with God! The Divine Fire is the offering, and the Light is the Offering; I am One with God! The Light of Wisdom is the Offering, and the Light is the Light of Wisdom; I am One with God!

(Wave light)

ॐ अग्निर्ज्योती रविर्ज्योतिश्चन्द्रो ज्योतिस्तथैव च ।

ज्योतिषामुत्तमो देव दीपोऽयं प्रतिगृह्यताम् ॥

एष दीपः ॐ नमः शिवाय ॥

oṃ agnirjyotī ravirjyotiścandro jyotistathaiva ca
jyotiṣāmuttamo deva dīpo-yaṃ pratigṛhyatām
eṣa dīpaḥ oṃ namaḥ śivāya

oṃ The Divine Fire is the Light, the Light of Wisdom is the Light, the Light of Devotion is the Light as well. The Light of the Highest Bliss, Oh God, is in the Light which we offer, the Light which we request you to accept. With the offering of Light oṃ I bow to the Consciousness of Infinite Goodness.

(Wave incense)

ॐ वनस्पतिरसोत्पन्नो गन्धात्ययी गन्ध उत्तमः ।

आघ्रेयः सर्वदेवानां धूपोऽयं प्रतिगृह्यताम् ॥

एष धूपः ॐ नमः शिवाय ॥

oṃ vanaspatirasotpanno
gandhātyayī gandha uttamaḥ
āghreyaḥ sarvadevānāṃ dhūpo-yaṃ pratigṛhyatām
eṣa dhūpaḥ oṃ namaḥ śivāya

oṃ Spirit of the Forest, from you is produced the most excellent of scents. The scent most pleasing to all the Gods, that scent we request you to accept. With the offering of fragrant scent oṃ I bow to the Consciousness of Infinite Goodness.

ārātrikam

ॐ चन्द्रादित्यौ च धरणी विद्युदग्निस्तथैव च ।

त्वमेव सर्वज्योतीषिं आरात्रिकं प्रतिगृह्यताम् ॥

ॐ नमः शिवाय आरात्रिकं समर्पयामि

oṃ candrādityau ca dharaṇī vidyudagnistathaiva ca
tvameva sarvajyotīṣiṃ ārātrikaṃ pratigṛhyatām
oṃ namaḥ śivāya ārātrikaṃ samarpayāmi

All knowing as the Moon, the Sun and the Divine Fire, you alone are all light, and this light we request you to accept. With the offering of light oṃ I bow to the Consciousness of Infinite Goodness.

ॐ पयः पृथिव्यां पय ओषधीषु
पयो दिव्यन्तरिक्षे पयो धाः ।
पयःस्वतीः प्रदिशः सन्तु मह्यम् ॥

oṃ payaḥ pṛthivyāṃ paya oṣadhīṣu
payo divyantarikṣe payo dhāḥ
payaḥsvatīḥ pradiśaḥ santu mahyam

oṃ Earth is a reservoir of nectar, all vegetation is a reservoir of nectar, the divine atmosphere is a reservoir of nectar, and also above. May all perceptions shine forth with the sweet taste of nectar for us.

ॐ अग्निर्देवता वातो देवता सूर्यो देवता चन्द्रमा देवता
वसवो देवता रुद्रो देवता ऽदित्या देवता मरुतो देवता विश्वे
देवा देवता बृहस्पतिर्देवतेन्द्रो देवता वरुणो देवता ॥

oṃ agnirdevatā vāto devatā sūryo devatā candramā
devatā vasavo devatā rudro devatā-dityā devatā
maruto devatā viśve devā devatā
bṛhaspatirdevatendro devatā varuṇo devatā

oṃ The Divine Fire (Light of Purity) is the shining God, the Wind is the shining God, the Sun (Light of Wisdom) is the shining God, the Moon (Lord of Devotion) is the shining God, the Protectors of the Wealth are the shining Gods, the Relievers of Sufferings are the shining Gods, the Sons of the Light are the shining Gods; the Emancipated seers (Maruts) are the shining Gods, the Universal Shining Gods are the shining Gods, the Guru of the Gods is the shining God, the Ruler of the Gods is the shining God, the Lord of Waters is the shining God.

ॐ भूर्भुवः स्वः ।
तत् सवितुर्वरेण्यम् भर्गो देवस्य धीमहि ।
धियो यो नः प्रचोदयात् ॥

oṃ bhūr bhuvaḥ svaḥ
tat savitur vareṇyam bhargo devasya dhīmahi
dhiyo yo naḥ pracodayāt

oṃ the Infinite Beyond Conception, the gross body, the subtle body and the causal body; we meditate upon that Light of Wisdom which is the Supreme Wealth of the Gods. May it grant to us increase in our meditations.

ॐ भूः

oṃ bhūḥ

oṃ the gross body

ॐ भुवः

oṃ bhuvaḥ

oṃ the subtle body

ॐ स्वः

oṃ svaḥ

oṃ the causal body

ॐ महः

oṃ mahaḥ

oṃ the great body of existence

ॐ जनः

oṃ janaḥ

oṃ the body of knowledge

ॐ तपः

oṃ tapaḥ
oṃ the body of light

ॐ सत्यं

oṃ satyaṃ
oṃ the body of Truth

ॐ तत् सवितुर्वरेण्यम् भर्गो देवस्य धीमहि ।
धियो यो नः प्रचोदयात् ॥

oṃ tat savitur vareṇyam bhargo devasya dhīmahi dhiyo yo naḥ pracodayāt
oṃ we meditate upon that Light of Wisdom which is the Supreme Wealth of the Gods. May it grant to us increase in our meditations.

ॐ आपो ज्योतीरसोमृतं ब्रह्म भूर्भुवस्स्वरोम् ॥

oṃ āpo jyotīrasomṛtaṃ brahma bhūrbhuvassvarom
May the divine waters luminous with the nectar of immortality of Supreme Divinity fill the earth, the atmosphere and the heavens.

ॐ मां माले महामाये सर्वशक्तिस्वरूपिणि ।
चतुर्वर्गस्त्वयि न्यस्तस्तस्मान्मे सिद्धिदा भव ॥

oṃ māṃ māle mahāmāye sarvaśaktisvarūpiṇi
catur vargas tvayi nyastas
tasmān me siddhidā bhava
oṃ My Rosary, the Great Measurement of Consciousness, containing all energy within as your intrinsic nature, give to me the attainment of your Perfection, fulfilling the four objectives of life.

ॐ अविघ्नं कुरु माले त्वं गृह्णामि दक्षिणे करे ।

जपकाले च सिद्ध्यर्थं प्रसीद मम सिद्धये ॥

oṃ avighnaṃ kuru māle tvaṃ
gṛhṇāmi dakṣiṇe kare
japakāle ca siddhyarthaṃ prasīda mama siddhaye

oṃ Rosary, You please remove all obstacles. I hold you in my right hand. At the time of recitation be pleased with me. Allow me to attain the Highest Perfection.

ॐ अक्षमालाधिपतये सुसिद्धिं देहि देहि

सर्वमन्त्रार्थसाधिनि साधय साधय सर्वसिद्धिं परिकल्पय

परिकल्पय मे स्वाहा ॥

oṃ akṣa mālā dhipataye susiddhiṃ dehi dehi sarva mantrārtha sādhini sādhaya sādhaya sarva siddhiṃ parikalpaya parikalpaya me svāhā

oṃ Rosary of rudrākṣa seeds, my Lord, give to me excellent attainment. Give to me, give to me. Illuminate the meanings of all mantras, illuminate, illuminate! Fashion me with all excellent attainments, fashion me! I am One with God!

एते गन्धपुष्पे ॐ गं गणपतये नमः

ete gandhapuṣpe oṃ gaṃ gaṇapataye namaḥ

With these scented flowers oṃ we bow to the Lord of Wisdom, Lord of the Multitudes.

एते गन्धपुष्पे ॐ आदित्यादिनवग्रहेभ्यो नमः

ete gandhapuṣpe oṃ ādityādi navagrahebhyo namaḥ

With these scented flowers oṃ we bow to the Sun, the Light of Wisdom, along with the nine planets.

एते गन्धपुष्पे ॐ शिवादिपञ्चदेवताभ्यो नमः

ete gandhapuṣpe oṃ śivādipañcadevatābhyo namaḥ

With these scented flowers oṃ we bow to Śiva, the Consciousness of Infinite Goodness, along with the five primary deities (Śiva, Śakti, Viṣṇu, Gaṇeśa, Sūrya).

एते गन्धपुष्पे ॐ इन्द्रादिदशदिक्पालेभ्यो नमः

ete gandhapuṣpe oṃ indrādi daśadikpālebhyo namaḥ

With these scented flowers oṃ we bow to Indra, the Ruler of the Pure, along with the Ten Protectors of the ten directions.

एते गन्धपुष्पे ॐ मत्स्यादिदशावतारेभ्यो नमः

ete gandhapuṣpe oṃ matsyādi daśāvatārebhyo namaḥ

With these scented flowers oṃ we bow to Viṣṇu, the Fish, along with the Ten Incarnations which He assumed.

एते गन्धपुष्पे ॐ प्रजापतये नमः

ete gandhapuṣpe oṃ prajāpataye namaḥ

With these scented flowers oṃ we bow to the Lord of All Created Beings.

एते गन्धपुष्पे ॐ नमो नारायणाय नमः

ete gandhapuṣpe oṃ namo nārāyaṇāya namaḥ

With these scented flowers oṃ we bow to the Perfect Perception of Consciousness.

एते गन्धपुष्पे ॐ सर्वेभ्यो देवेभ्यो नमः

ete gandhapuṣpe oṃ sarvebhyo devebhyo namaḥ

With these scented flowers oṃ we bow to All the Gods.

एते गन्धपुष्पे ॐ सर्वाभ्यो देवीभ्यो नमः

ete gandhapuṣpe oṃ sarvābhyo devībhyo namaḥ

With these scented flowers oṃ we bow to All the Goddesses.

एते गन्धपुष्पे ॐ श्री गुरवे नमः

ete gandhapuṣpe oṃ śrī gurave namaḥ

With these scented flowers oṃ we bow to the Guru.

एते गन्धपुष्पे ॐ ब्राह्मणेभ्यो नमः

ete gandhapuṣpe oṃ brāhmaṇebhyo namaḥ

With these scented flowers oṃ we bow to All Knowers of Wisdom.

Tie a piece of string around right middle finger or wrist.

ॐ कुशासने स्थितो ब्रह्मा कुशे चैव जनार्दनः ।
कुशे ह्याकाशवद् विष्णुः कुशासन नमोऽस्तु ते ॥

oṃ kuśāsane sthito brahmā kuśe caiva janārdanaḥ
kuśe hyākāśavad viṣṇuḥ kuśāsana namo-stu te

Brahmā is in the shining light (or kuśa grass), in the shining light resides Janārdana, the Lord of Beings. The Supreme all-pervading Consciousness, Viṣṇu, resides in the shining light. Oh Repository of the shining light, we bow down to you, the seat of kuśa grass.

आचमन

ācamana

ॐ केशवाय नमः स्वाहा

oṃ keśavāya namaḥ svāhā

We bow to the one of beautiful hair.

ॐ माधवाय नमः स्वाहा

oṃ mādhavāya namaḥ svāhā
We bow to the one who is always sweet.

ॐ गोविन्दाय नमः स्वाहा

oṃ govindāya namaḥ svāhā
We bow to He who is one-pointed light.

ॐ विष्णुः ॐ विष्णुः ॐ विष्णुः

oṃ viṣṇuḥ oṃ viṣṇuḥ oṃ viṣṇuḥ
oṃ Consciousness, oṃ Consciousness, oṃ Consciousness.

ॐ तत् विष्णोः परमं पदम् सदा पश्यन्ति सूरयः ।

दिवीव चक्षुराततम् ॥

oṃ tat viṣṇoḥ paramaṃ padam
sadā paśyanti sūrayaḥ
divīva cakṣurā tatam
oṃ That Consciousness of the highest station, who always sees the Light of Wisdom, give us Divine Eyes.

ॐ तद् विप्र स पिपानोव जुविग्रन्सो सोमिन्द्रते ।

विष्णुः तत् परमं पदम् ॥

oṃ tad vipra sa pipānova juvigranso somindrate
viṣṇuḥ tat paramaṃ padam
oṃ That twice-born teacher who is always thirsty for accepting the nectar of devotion, Oh Consciousness, you are in that highest station.

ॐ अपवित्रः पवित्रो वा सर्वावस्थां गतोऽपि वा ।
यः स्मरेत् पुण्डरीकाक्षं स बाह्याभ्यन्तरः शुचिः ॥

oṃ apavitraḥ pavitro vā sarvāvasthāṃ gato-pi vā
yaḥ smaret puṇḍarīkākṣaṃ
sa bāhyābhyantaraḥ śuciḥ

oṃ The Impure and the Pure reside within all objects. Who remembers the lotus-eyed Consciousness is conveyed to radiant beauty.

ॐ सर्वमङ्गलमाङ्गल्यम् वरेण्यम् वरदं शुभं ।
नारायणं नमस्कृत्य सर्वकर्माणि कारयेत् ॥

oṃ sarva maṅgala māṅgalyam
vareṇyam varadaṃ śubhaṃ
nārāyaṇaṃ namaskṛtya sarvakarmāṇi kārayet

All the Welfare of all Welfare, the highest blessing of Purity and Illumination, with the offering of respect we bow down to the Supreme Consciousness who is the actual performer of all action.

ॐ सूर्य्यश्चमेति मन्त्रस्य ब्रह्मा ऋषिः प्रकृतिश्छन्दः आपो देवता आचमने विनियोगः ॥

oṃ sūryyaścameti mantrasya brahmā ṛṣiḥ
prakṛtiśchandaḥ āpo devatā ācamane viniyogaḥ

oṃ These are the mantras of the Light of Wisdom, the Creative Capacity is the Seer, Nature is the meter, the divine flow of waters is the deity, being applied in washing the hands and rinsing the mouth.

Draw the following yantra with some drops of water and/or sandal paste at the front of your seat.
Place a flower on the bindu in the middle.

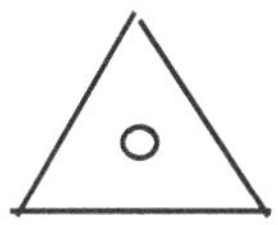

ॐ आसनस्य मन्त्रस्य मेरुपृष्ठ ऋषिः सुतलं छन्दः कूर्म्मो देवता आसनोपवेशने विनियोगः ॥

oṃ āsanasya mantrasya merupṛṣṭha ṛṣiḥ sutalaṃ chandaḥ kūrmmo devatā āsanopaveśane viniyogaḥ

Introducing the mantras of the Purification of the seat. The Seer is He whose back is Straight, the meter is of very beautiful form, the tortoise who supports the earth is the deity. These mantras are applied to make the seat free from obstructions.

एते गन्धपुष्पे ॐ ह्रीं आधारशक्तये कमलासनाय नमः ॥

ete gandhapuṣpe oṃ hrīṃ ādhāraśaktaye kamalāsanāya namaḥ

With these scented flowers oṃ hrīṃ we bow to the Primal Energy situated in this lotus seat.

ॐ पृथ्वि त्वया धृता लोका देवि त्वं विष्णुना धृता ।
त्वञ्च धारय मां नित्यं पवित्रं कुरु चासनम् ॥

oṃ pṛthvi tvayā dhṛtā lokā devi tvaṃ viṣṇunā dhṛtā tvañca dhāraya māṃ nityaṃ pavitraṃ kuru cāsanam

oṃ Earth! You support the realms of the Goddess. You are supported by the Supreme Consciousness. Also bear me eternally and make pure this seat.

ॐ गुरुभ्यो नमः

oṃ gurubhyo namaḥ
oṃ I bow to the Guru.

ॐ परमगुरुभ्यो नमः

oṃ paramagurubhyo namaḥ
oṃ I bow to the Guru's Guru.

ॐ परापरगुरुभ्यो नमः

oṃ parāparagurubhyo namaḥ
oṃ I bow to the Gurus of the lineage.

ॐ परमेष्ठिगुरुभ्यो नमः

oṃ parameṣṭhigurubhyo namaḥ
oṃ I bow to the Supreme Gurus.

ॐ गं गणेशाय नमः

oṃ gaṃ gaṇeśāya namaḥ
oṃ I bow to the Lord of Wisdom.

ॐ अनन्ताय नमः

oṃ anantāya namaḥ
oṃ I bow to the Infinite One.

ॐ ऐं ह्रीं क्लीं चामुण्डायै विच्चे

oṃ aiṃ hrīṃ klīṃ cāmuṇḍāyai vicce
oṃ Creation, Circumstance, Transformation are known by Consciousness.

ॐ नमः शिवाय

oṃ namaḥ śivāya
oṃ I bow to the Consciousness of Infinite Goodness.

Clap hands 3 times and snap fingers in the ten directions (N S E W NE SW NW SE UP DOWN) repeating

ॐ नमः शिवाय

oṃ namaḥ śivāya
oṃ I bow to the Consciousness of Infinite Goodness.

सङ्कल्प

sankalpa

विष्णुः ॐ तत् सत् । ॐ अद्य जम्बूद्वीपे ( ) देशे ( ) प्रदेशे ( ) नगरे ( ) मन्दिरे ( ) मासे ( ) पक्षे ( ) तिथौ ( ) गोत्र श्री ( ) कृतैतत् श्रीशिवकामः पूजाकर्माहं श्रीशुक्ल यजुर्वेदीय रुद्राष्टाध्यायी करिष्ये ॥

viṣṇuḥ oṃ tat sat oṃ adya jambūdvīpe (Country) deśe (State) pradeśe (City) nagare (Name of house or temple) mandire (month) māse (śukla or kṛṣṇa) pakṣe (name of day) tithau (name of) gotra śrī (your name) kṛtaitat śrī śiva kāmaḥ pūjā karmāhaṃ śrī śukla yajurvedīya rudrāṣṭādhyāyī kariṣye

The Consciousness Which Pervades All, oṃ That is Truth. Presently, on the Planet Earth, Country of (Name), State of (Name), City of (Name), in the Temple of (Name), (Name of Month) Month, (Bright or Dark) fortnight, (Name of Day) Day, (Name of Sādhu Family), Śrī (Your Name) is performing the worship for the satisfaction of the Respected Consciousness of Infinite Goodness by reciting the Eight Chapters in Praise of Rudra from the bright portion of the Yajur Veda.

ॐ यज्जाग्रतो दूरमुदेति दैवं तदु सुप्तस्य तथैवैति ।
दूरङ्गमं ज्योतिषां ज्योतिरेकं तन्मे मनः शिवसङ्कल्पमस्तु ॥

oṃ yajjāgrato dūramudeti
daivaṃ tadu suptasya tathaivaiti
dūraṅgamaṃ jyotiṣāṃ jyotirekaṃ
tanme manaḥ śiva saṅkalpamastu

May our waking consciousness replace pain and suffering with divinity as also our awareness when asleep. Far extending be our radiant aura of light, filling our minds with light. May that be the firm determination of the Consciousness of Infinite Goodness.

या गुङ्गूर्या सिनीवाली या राका या सरस्वती ।
ईन्द्राणीमह्व ऊतये वरुणानीं स्वस्तये ॥

yā guṅgūryā sinīvālī yā rākā yā sarasvatī
īndrāṇīmahva ūtaye varuṇānīṃ svastaye

May that Goddess who wears the Moon of Devotion protect the children of Devotion. May that Goddess of All-Pervading Knowledge protect us. May the Energy of the Rule of the Pure rise up. Oh Energy of Equilibrium grant us the highest prosperity.

ॐ स्वस्ति न इन्द्रो वृद्धश्रवाः स्वस्ति नः पूषा विश्ववेदाः ।
स्वस्ति नस्ताक्ष्र्यो अरिष्टनेमिः स्वस्ति नो बृहस्पतिर्दधातु ॥

oṃ svasti na indro vṛddhaśravāḥ
svasti naḥ pūṣā viśvavedāḥ
svasti nastārkṣyo ariṣṭanemiḥ
svasti no bṛhaspatirdadhātu

The Ultimate Prosperity to us, Oh Rule of the Pure, who perceives all that changes; the Ultimate Prosperity to us, Searchers for Truth, Knowers of the Universe; the Ultimate

Prosperity to us, Oh Divine Being of Light, keep us safe; the Ultimate Prosperity to us, Oh Spirit of All-Pervading Delight, grant that to us.

ॐ गणानां त्वा गणपति᳖ हवामहे

प्रियाणां त्वा प्रियपति᳖ हवामहे

निधीनां त्वा निधिपति᳖ हवामहे वसो मम ।

आहमजानि गर्ब्भधमा त्वमजासि गर्ब्भधम् ॥

oṃ gaṇānāṃ tvā gaṇapati guṃ havāmahe
priyāṇāṃ tvā priyapati guṃ havāmahe
nidhīnāṃ tvā nidhipati guṃ havāmahe vaso mama
āhamajāni garbbhadhamā tvamajāsi garbbhadham

We invoke you with offerings, Oh Lord of the Multitudes; we invoke you with offerings, Oh Lord of Love; we invoke you with offerings, Oh Guardian of the Treasure. Sit within me, giving birth to the realm of the Gods within me; yes, giving birth to the realm of the Gods within me.

ॐ गणानां त्वा गणपति᳖ हवामहे

कविं कवीनामुपमश्रवस्तमम् ।

ज्येष्ठराजं ब्रह्मणां ब्रह्मणस्पत

आ नः शृण्वन्नूतिभिः सीद सादनम् ॥

oṃ gaṇānāṃ tvā gaṇapati guṃ havāmahe
kaviṃ kavīnāmupamaśravastamam
jyeṣṭharājaṃ brahmaṇāṃ brahmaṇaspata
ā naḥ śṛṇvannūtibhiḥ sīda sādanam

We invoke you with offerings, Oh Lord of the Multitudes, Seer among Seers, of unspeakable grandeur. Oh Glorious King, Lord of the Knowers of Wisdom, come speedily hearing our supplications and graciously take your seat amidst our assembly.

ॐ अदितिर्द्यौरदितिरन्तरिक्षमदितिर्माता स पिता स पुत्रः । विश्वे देवा अदितिः पञ्च जना अदितिर्जातमदितिर्जनित्वम् ॥

oṃ aditir dyauraditirantarikṣam
aditirmātā sa pitā sa putraḥ
viśve devā aditiḥ pañca janā
aditirjātamaditirjanitvam

The Mother of Enlightenment pervades the heavens; the Mother of Enlightenment pervades the atmosphere; the Mother of Enlightenment pervades Mother and Father and child. All Gods of the Universe are pervaded by the Mother, the five forms of living beings, all Life. The Mother of Enlightenment, She is to be known.

ॐ त्वं स्त्रीस्त्वं पुमानसि त्वं कुमार अत वा कुमारी ।
त्वं जिर्नो दण्डेन वञ्चसि त्वं जातो भवसि विश्वतोमुखः ॥

oṃ tvaṃ strīstvaṃ pumānasi
tvaṃ kumāra ata vā kumarī
tvaṃ jirno daṇḍena vañcasi
tvaṃ jāto bhavasi viśvatomukhaḥ

You are Female, you are Male; you are a young boy, you are a young girl. You are the word of praise by which we are singing; you are all creation existing as the mouth of the universe.

ॐ अम्बेऽम्बिकेऽम्बालिके न मा नयति कश्चन ।
ससस्त्यश्वकः सुभद्रिकां काम्पीलवासिनीम् ॥

oṃ ambe-ambike-mbālike na mā nayati kaścana
sasastyaśvakaḥ subhadrikāṃ kāmpīlavāsinīm

Mother of the Perceivable Universe, Mother of the Conceivable Universe, Mother of the Universe of Intuitive Vision, lead me to that True Existence. As excellent crops (or grains) are harvested, so may I be taken to reside with the Infinite Consciousness.

ॐ शान्ता द्यौः शान्तापृथिवी शान्तमिदमुर्वन्तरिक्षम् ।
शान्ता उदन्वतिरापः शान्ताः नः शान्त्वोषधीः ॥

oṃ śāntā dyauḥ śāntā pṛthivī
śāntam idamurvantarikṣam
śāntā udanvatirāpaḥ śāntāḥ naḥ śāntvoṣadhīḥ

Peace in the heavens, Peace on the earth, Peace upwards and permeating the atmosphere; Peace upwards, over, on all sides and further; Peace to us, Peace to all vegetation;

ॐ शान्तानि पूर्वरूपाणि शान्तं नोऽस्तु कृताकृतम् ।
शान्तं भूतं च भव्यं च सर्वमेव शमस्तु नः ॥

oṃ śāntāni pūrva rūpāṇi śāntaṃ no-stu kṛtākṛtam
śāntaṃ bhūtaṃ ca bhavyaṃ ca sarvameva śamastu naḥ

Peace to all that has form, Peace to all causes and effects; Peace to all existence, and to all intensities of reality including all and everything; Peace be to us.

ॐ पृथिवी शान्तिरन्तरिक्षं शान्तिर्द्यौः
शान्तिरापः शान्तिरोषधयः शान्तिः वनस्पतयः शान्तिर्विश्वे
मे देवाः शान्तिः सर्वे मे देवाः शान्तिर्ब्रह्म शान्तिरापः
शान्तिः सर्वं शान्तिरेधि शान्तिः शान्तिः सर्व शान्तिः
सा मा शान्तिः शान्तिभिः ॥

oṃ pṛthivī śāntir antarikṣaṃ śāntir dyauḥ śāntir āpaḥ śāntir oṣadhayaḥ śāntiḥ vanaspatayaḥ śāntir viśve me devāḥ śāntiḥ sarve me devāḥ śāntir brahma śāntirāpaḥ śāntiḥ sarvaṃ śāntiredhi śāntiḥ śāntiḥ sarva śāntiḥ sā mā śāntiḥ śāntibhiḥ

Let the earth be at Peace, the atmosphere be at Peace, the heavens be filled with Peace. Even further may Peace extend, Peace be to waters, Peace to all vegetation, Peace to All Gods of the Universe, Peace to All Gods within us, Peace to Creative Consciousness, Peace be to Brilliant Light, Peace to All, Peace to Everything, Peace, Peace, altogether Peace, equally Peace, by means of Peace.

ताभिः शान्तिभिः सर्वशान्तिभिः समया मोहं यदिह घोरं यदिह क्रूरं यदिह पापं तच्छान्तं तच्छिवं सर्वमेव समस्तु नः ॥

tābhiḥ śāntibhiḥ sarva śāntibhiḥ samayā mohaṃ yadiha ghoraṃ yadiha krūraṃ yadiha pāpaṃ tacchāntaṃ tacchivaṃ sarvameva samastu naḥ

Thus by means of Peace, altogether one with the means of Peace, Ignorance is eliminated, Violence is eradicated, Improper Conduct is eradicated, Confusion (sin) is eradicated, all that is, is at Peace, all that is perceived, each and everything, altogether for us,

ॐ शान्तिः शान्तिः शान्तिः ॥

oṃ śāntiḥ śāntiḥ śāntiḥ

oṃ Peace, Peace, Peace

ॐ ध्यायेन्नित्यं महेशं रजतगिरिनिभं चारुचन्द्रावतंसं
रत्ना कल्पोज्वलांगं परशु मृगवयाभीति हस्तं प्रसन्नं ।
पद्मासीनं समन्तात् स्तुतऽममरगणैर्व्याघ्रकृत्तिं वसानं
विश्वाद्यं विश्वबीजं निखलभयहरं पञ्चवक्त्रं त्रिनेत्रं ॥

oṃ dhyāyen nityaṃ maheśaṃ
rajata girinibhaṃ cāru candrā vataṃsaṃ
ratnā kalpo jvalāṃgaṃ
paraśu mṛga vayābhīti hastaṃ prasannaṃ
padmāsīnaṃ samantāt
stuta-mama raganair vyāghra kṛtiṃ vasānaṃ
viśvādyaṃ viśva bījaṃ
nikhala bhayaharaṃ pañca vaktraṃ trinetraṃ

oṃ We always meditate on He who shines like the white mountains, ornamented by a digit of the moon on His head. His body shines like jewels. In His left hands He displays an axe and the Mṛga Mudrā (Kalpataru Mudrā, with the thumb, middle and ring fingers joined with the pointer and pinky extended up) and in His two right hands He shows mudrās granting blessings and fearlessness. He is of beautiful appearance seated in the full lotus asana. On His four sides the Gods are present singing hymns of praise. His wearing apparel is a tiger's skin. He is before the universe and the cause of the universe. He removes all fear, has five faces and three eyes.

kara nyāsa
establishment in the hands

ॐ नं अंगुष्ठाभ्यां नमः

oṃ naṃ aṅguṣṭhābhyāṃ namaḥ thumb forefinger
oṃ naṃ in the thumb I bow.

ॐ मः तर्जनीभ्यां स्वाहा

oṃ maḥ tarjanībhyāṃ svāhā thumb forefinger
oṃ maḥ in the forefinger, I am One with God!

ॐ शिं मध्यमाभ्यां वषट्

oṃ śiṃ madhyamābhyāṃ vaṣaṭ thumb middle finger
oṃ śiṃ in the middle finger, Purify!

ॐ वां अनामिकाभ्यां हुं

oṃ vāṃ anāmikābhyāṃ huṃ thumb ring finger
oṃ vāṃ in the ring finger, Cut the Ego!

ॐ यः कनिष्ठिकाभ्यां वौषट्

oṃ yaḥ kaniṣṭhikābhyāṃ vauṣaṭ thumb little finger
oṃ yaḥ in the little finger, Ultimate Purity!

Roll hand over hand forwards while reciting karatala kara and backwards while chanting pṛṣṭhābhyāṃ, then clap hands when chanting astrāya phaṭ.

ॐ नमः शिवाय करतल कर पृष्ठाभ्यां अस्त्राय फट् ॥

oṃ namaḥ śivāya karatala kara pṛṣṭhābhyāṃ astrāya phaṭ
oṃ I bow to the Consciousness of Infinite Goodness with the weapon of Virtue.

ॐ नमः शिवाय

oṃ namaḥ śivāya
oṃ I bow to the Consciousness of Infinite Goodness.

aṅga nyāsa
establishment in the body

Holding tattva mudrā, touch heart.

ॐ नं हृदयाय नमः

oṃ naṃ hṛdayāya namaḥ touch heart
oṃ naṃ in the heart, I bow.

Holding tattva mudrā touch top of head.

ॐ मः शिरसे स्वाहा

oṃ maḥ śirase svāhā top of head
oṃ maḥ on the top of the head, I am One with God!

With thumb extended, touch back of head.

ॐ शिं शिखायै वषट्

oṃ śiṃ śikhāyai vaṣaṭ back of head
oṃ śiṃ on the back of the head, Purify!

Holding tattva mudrā, cross both arms.

ॐ वां कवचाय हुं

oṃ vāṃ kavacāya huṃ cross both arms
oṃ vāṃ crossing both arms, Cut the Ego!

Holding tattva mudrā, touch three eyes at once with three middle fingers.

ॐ यः नेत्रत्रयाय वौषट्

oṃ yaḥ netratrayāya vauṣaṭ touch three eyes
oṃ yaḥ in the three eyes, Ultimate Purity!

Roll hand over hand forwards while reciting karatala kara and backwards while chanting pṛṣṭhābhyāṃ, then clap hands when chanting astrāya phaṭ.

ॐ नमः शिवाय करतल कर पृष्ठाभ्यां अस्त्राय फट् ॥

oṃ namaḥ śivāya karatala kara pṛṣṭhābhyāṃ astrāya phaṭ

oṃ I bow to the Consciousness of Infinite Goodness with the weapon of Virtue.

ॐ नमः शिवाय

oṃ namaḥ śivāya

oṃ I bow to the Consciousness of Infinite Goodness.

(108 times)

Chapter 1

ॐ नमः पार्वतीपते

oṃ namaḥ pārvatīpate
oṃ I bow to the husband of Pārvatī.

हरिः ॐ

hariḥ oṃ
Praise to oṃ

- 1 -

ॐ गणानां त्वा गणपति(ँ) हवामहे
प्रियाणां त्वा प्रियपति(ँ) हवामहे
निधीनां त्वा निधिपति(ँ) हवामहे वसो मम ।
आहमजानि गर्ब्भधमा त्वमजासि गर्ब्भधम् ॥

oṃ gaṇānāṃ tvā gaṇapati guṃ havāmahe
priyāṇāṃ tvā priyapati guṃ havāmahe
nidhīnāṃ tvā nidhipati guṃ havāmahe vaso mama
āhamajāni garbbhadhamā tvamajāsi garbbhadham

We invoke you with offerings, Oh Lord of the Multitudes; we invoke you with offerings, Oh Lord of Love; we invoke you with offerings, Oh Guardian of the Treasure. Sit within me, giving birth to the realm of the Gods within me; yes, giving birth to the realm of the Gods within me.

- 2 -

गायत्री त्रिष्टुब्जगत्यनुष्टुप्पङ्क्त्या सह ।
बृहत्युष्णिहा ककुप्सूचीभिः शम्यन्तु त्वा ॥

gāyatrī triṣṭubjagatyanuṣṭuppaṅktyā saha
bṛhatyuṣṇihā kakupsūcībhiḥ śamyantu tvā

We are reciting with the Saṃskṛta meters gāyatrī, triṣṭup, jagati, anuṣṭup, paṅkti, bṛhati, uṣṇig, and kakup, which have been demonstrated to bring you peace.

\- 3 -

द्विपदा याश्चतुष्पदास्त्रिपदा याश्च षट्पदाः ।

विच्छन्दा याश्च सच्छन्दाः सूचीभिः सम्यन्तु त्वा ॥

dvipadā yāścatuṣpadāstripadā yāśca ṣaṭpadāḥ
vicchandā yāśca sacchandāḥ sūcībhiḥ samyantu tvā

We are reciting with two syllables and with four syllables, with three syllables and with six syllables, without meter and with meter as has been indicated to bring you peace.

\- 4 -

सहस्तोमाः सहच्छन्दस आवृतः

सहप्रमा ऋषयः सप्त दैव्याः ।

पूर्वेषां पन्थामनुदृश्य धीरा अन्वलेभिरे रथ्यो न रश्मीन् ॥

sahastomāḥ sahacchandasa āvṛtaḥ sahapramā
ṛṣayaḥ sapta daivyāḥ
pūrveṣāṃ panthāmanudṛśya dhīrā anvalebhire
rathyo na raśamīn

In ancient times the seven ṛṣis understood the path by which to return to divinity, by consistently perceiving that the natural order of the mind is united with hymns and meters.

\- 5 -

यज्जाग्रतो दूरमुदैति दैवं तदु सुप्तस्य तथैवेति ।

दूरंगमं ज्योतिषां ज्योतिरेकं तन्मे मनः शिवसंकल्पमस्तु ॥

yajjāgrato dūramudaiti daivaṃ
tadu suptasya tathaiveti
dūraṃgamaṃ jyotiṣāṃ jyotirekaṃ
tanme manaḥ śivasaṃkalpamastu

May our waking consciousness replace pain and suffering with divinity, as also our awareness when asleep. May our radiant aura of light extend far, filling our minds with light. May my mind be filled with that firm determination of Śiva, the Consciousness of Infinite Goodness.

- 6 -

येन कर्माण्यपसो मनीषिणो

यज्ञे कृण्वन्ति विदथेषु धीराः ।

यदपूर्वं यक्षमन्तः प्रजानां तन्मे मनः शिवसंकल्पमस्तु ॥

yena karmāṇyapaso manīṣiṇo
yajñe kṛṇvanti vidatheṣu dhīrāḥ
yadapūrvaṃ yakṣamantaḥ prajānāṃ
tanme manaḥ śivasaṃkalpamastu

The excellent actions of thinking beings, steadfastly offering their knowledge in sacrificial union, is the ancient means of enhancing the wealth of the people. May my mind be filled with that firm determination of Śiva, the Consciousness of Infinite Goodness.

- 7 -

यत् प्रज्ञानमुत चेतो धृतिश्च यज्ज्योतिरन्तरमृतं प्रजासु ।

यस्मान्न ऋते किञ्चन कर्म क्रियते

तन्मे मनः शिवसंकल्पमस्तु ॥

yat prajñānamuta ceto dhṛtiśca
yajjyotirantaramṛtaṃ prajāsu
yasmānna ṛte kiñcana karma kriyate
tanme manaḥ śivasaṃkalpamastu

Being firm in that supreme wisdom which fills consciousness, that inner light of the nectar of bliss within all beings born, may we perform all actions from that imperishable truth. May my mind be filled with that firm determination of Śiva, the Consciousness of Infinite Goodness.

- 8 -

येनेदं भूतं भुवनं भविष्यत् परि गृहीतममृतेन सर्वम् ।

येन यज्ञस्तायते सप्तहोता तन्मे मनः शिवसंकल्पमस्तु ॥

yenedaṃ bhūtaṃ bhuvanaṃ bhaviṣyat
pari gṛhītamamṛtena sarvam
yena yajñastāyate saptahotā
tanme manaḥ śivasaṃkalpamastu

By means of this supreme wisdom all beings in the manifested worlds of the future will be able to completely dwell with the nectar of immortal bliss, by means of the sacrificial fire attended by seven offerings on seven levels of consciousness. May my mind be filled with that firm determination of Śiva, the Consciousness of Infinite Goodness.

- 9 -

यस्मिन्नृचः साम यजूंषि यस्मिन्
प्रतिष्ठिता रथनाभाविवाराः ।
यस्मिंश्चित्तं सर्वमोतं प्रजानां तन्मे मनः शिवसंकल्पमस्तु ॥

yasminnṛcaḥ sāma yajūṃṣi yasmin
pratiṣṭhitā rathanābhāvivārāḥ
yasmiṃścittaṃ sarvamotaṃ prajānāṃ
tanme manaḥ śivasaṃkalpamastu

This is where the Ṛg, Sāma and Yajūr Vedas have been established, the conveyance of the great attitude; from where all the highest contemplations of all life emanate. May my mind be filled with that firm determination of Śiva, the Consciousness of Infinite Goodness.

- 10 -

सुषारथिरश्वानिव यन्मनुष्यान्
नेनीयतेऽभीशुभिर्वाजिन इव ।
हृत्प्रतिष्ठं यदजिरं यविष्ठं तन्मे मनः शिवसंकल्पमस्तु ॥

suṣārathiraśvāniva yanmanuṣyān
nenīyate-bhīśubhirvājina iva
hṛtpratiṣṭhaṃ yadajiraṃ yaviṣṭhaṃ
tanme manaḥ śivasaṃkalpamastu

He is the excellent charioteer of the horses of mankind, awakening them from sloth and laziness to this renewed energy, established in delight for both the old and the young. May my mind be filled with that firm determination of Śiva, the Consciousness of Infinite Goodness.

इति प्रथमोऽध्यायः

iti prathamo-dhyāyaḥ
Thus ends the first chapter.

Chapter 2

हरिः ॐ

hariḥ oṃ

Praise to oṃ

\- 1 -

सहस्रशीर्षा पुरुषः सहस्राक्षः सहस्रपात् ।

स भूमिं सर्व तस्पृत्वाऽत्यतिष्ठद्दशाङ्गुलम् ॥

sahasraśīrṣā puruṣaḥ sahasrākṣaḥ sahasrapāt
sa bhūmiṃ sarva taspṛtvā-tyatiṣṭhaddaśāṅgulām

The full, complete and perfect consciousness has a thousand heads, a thousand eyes, a thousand feet. He pervades the earth and the space on every side, while He manifests in all aspects of the world of ten. (The place of ten fingers breadth, the heart; the world comprised of earth, water, fire, air, ether and smell, taste, sight, touch, sound; the world encompassed by the ten directions.)

\- 2 -

पुरुष एवेदं सर्वं यद्भूतं यच्च भाव्यम् ।

उतामृतत्वस्येशानो यदन्नेनातिरोहति ॥

puruṣa evedaṃ sarvaṃ yadbhūtaṃ yacca bhāvyam
utāmṛtatvasyeśāno yadannenātirohati

The full, complete and perfect consciousness alone has given birth to all that has become and all that will become. From Him comes all that is and all that dwells in immortal bliss.

\- 3 -

एतावानस्य महिमाऽतो ज्यायांश्च पूरुषः ।

पादोऽस्य विश्वा भूतानि त्रिपादस्यामृतं दिवि ॥

etāvānasya mahimā-to jyāyāṃśca pūruṣaḥ
pādo-sya viśvā bhūtāni tripādasyāmṛtaṃ divi

The full, complete and perfect consciousness demonstrates His greatness in the perceivable and the imperceptible. The entire universe is His one part, while three parts exist in the divinity of the nectar of immortal bliss.

- 4 -

त्रिपादूर्ध्व उदैत्पुरुषः पादोऽस्येहाभवत्पुनः ।

ततोविष्वं व्यक्रामत्साशनानशनेऽअभि ॥

tripādūrdhva udaitpuruṣaḥ pādo-syehābhavatpunaḥ
tatoviṣvaṃ vyakrāmatsāśanānaśane-abhi

The full, complete and perfect consciousness rises in the three parts above, while with the one part, He creates the entire creation again and again and resides within.

- 5 -

ततो विराडजायत विराजोऽअधि पूरुषः ।

सजातोऽअत्यरिच्यत पश्चाद्भूमिमथो पुरः ॥

tato virāḍajāyata virājo-adhi pūruṣaḥ
sajāto-atyaricyata paścādbhūmimātho puraḥ

The full, complete and perfect consciousness is the eternal master. He created the vast existence and thereafter the land.

- 6 -

तस्माद्यज्ञत्सवहुतः सम्भृतं पृषदाज्यम् ।

पशूंस्तांश्चक्रे वायव्यानारण्या ग्राम्याश्च ये ॥

tāsmādyjñatsavahutaḥ sambhṛtaṃ pṛṣadājyam
paśūṃstāṃścakre vāyavyānāraṇyā grāmyāścā ye

Then He created yajña, the sacrifice of attachment to duality through attentive offering, and then the animals of the forests, those who fly with the wind, and those who live in villages.

- 7 -

तस्माद्यज्ञात्सर्वहुतऽऋचः सामानि जज्ञिरे ।

छन्दांऽसि जज्ञिरे तस्माद्यजुस्तस्मादजायत ॥

tāsmādyajñātsarvahuta-ṛcaḥ sāmāni jajñire chandāṃ-si jajñire tasmādyajustasmādajāyata

Then from yajña hymns and songs and poetic meters became known. And then the Veda of sacrifice came forth.

\- 8 -

तस्मादश्वाऽअजायन्त ये के चोभयादतः ।

गावो ह जज्ञिरे तस्मात्तस्माज्जाताऽअजावयः ॥

tasmādaśvā-ajāyanta ye ke cobhayādataḥ gāvo ha jajñire tasmāttasmājjātā-ajāvayaḥ

Then came both horses and cows and all beings that take birth.

\- 9 -

तं यज्ञं बर्हिषि प्रौक्षन्पुरुषं जातमग्रतः ।

तेन देवाऽअयजन्त साध्याऽऋषयश्च ये ॥

taṃ yajñaṃ barhiṣi praukṣanpuruṣaṃ jātamagrataḥ tena devā-ayajanta sādhyā-ṛṣayaśca ye

The gods, pure beings, and ṛṣis know Him, the One who knows all, the full, complete and perfect consciousness by demonstrating respect in the yajña of sacrificial offerings.

\- 10 -

यत्पुरुषं व्यदधुः कतिधा व्यकल्पयन् ।

मखं किमस्यासीत्किं बाहू किमूरू पादाऽउच्येते ॥

yatpuruṣaṃ vyadadhuḥ katidhā vyakalpayan makhaṃ kimasyāsītkiṃ bāhū kimūrū pādā-ucyete

The full, complete, and perfect consciousness is so diverse, how varied are his descriptions. Who is represented by the head, who by the arms, who by the feet?

\- 11 -

ब्राह्मणोऽस्य मुखमासीद् बाहू राजन्यः कृतः ।

ऊरू तदस्य यद्वैश्यः पद्भ्यां शूद्रोऽअजायत ॥

brāhmaṇo-sya mukhamāsīd bāhū rājanyaḥ kṛtaḥ
ūrū tadasya yadvaiśyaḥ padbhyāṃ śūdro-ajāyata
From His head came the Knowers of Wisdom, from His arms kings and administrators. From His thighs came forth those of circulation and distribution, and from His feet support and sustenance[1].

- 12 -

चन्द्रमा मनसो जातश्चक्षोः सूर्यो ऽअजायत ।
श्रोत्राद्वायुश्च प्राणाणश्च मखादग्निरजायत ॥

candramā manaso jātaścakṣoḥ sūryo-ajāyata
śrotrādvāyuścā prāṇāṇaśca makhādagnirajāyata
His mind gave birth to the Moon, and His eyes gave birth to the Sun. From His ears and His breath came the Wind, and from His mouth came the Lord of Fire.

- 13 -

नाभ्भ्या ऽआसीदन्तरिक्षँ शीर्ष्णो द्यौः समवर्त्तत ।
पद्भ्यां भूमिर्द्दिशः श्रोत्रात्तथा लोकांऽअकल्पयन् ॥

nābbhyā-āsīdantarikṣaṁ śīrṣṇo dyauḥ samavarttata
padbhyāṃ bhūmirddiśaḥ śrotrāt
tathā lokāṃ-akalpayan
From His navel came forth the atmosphere, and from His head the heavens. From His feet came the earth, and from his ears the directions. Thus existence became manifested.

- 14 -

यत्पुरुषेण हविषा देवा यज्ञमतन्वत ।
वसन्तोऽस्यासीदाज्यं ग्रीष्मऽइध्मः शरद्धविः ॥

yatpuruṣeṇa haviṣā devā yajñamatanvata
vasanto-syāsīdājyaṃ grīṣma-īdhmaḥ śaraddhaviḥ
The Gods performed sacrifice with that Supreme Being as the offering. Spring was the clarified butter oil, summer the fuel and autumn the oblation.

- 15 -

सप्तास्यासन्परिधयस्त्रिः सप्त समिधः कृताः ।

देवा यद्यज्ञं तन्वानाऽअबध्नन्पुरुषं पशुम् ॥

saptāsyāsanparidhayastriḥ sapta samidhaḥ kṛtāḥ
devā yadyajñaṃ tanvānā-abadhnānpuruṣaṃ paśum

Seven were the limitations defined[2], three times seven, the ingedients used. When the Gods offered that sacrifice, they bound their animalistic nature and offered it to the Supreme Being.

- 16 -

यज्ञेन यज्ञमयजन्त देवास्तानि धर्म्माणि प्रथमान्यासन् ।

ते ह नाकं महिमानः सचन्त यत्र पूर्वे

साध्याः सन्ति देवाः ॥

yajñena yajñamayajanta devāstāni dharmmāṇi prathamānyāsan
te ha nākaṃ mahimānaḥ sacanta yatra pūrve sādhyāḥ santi devāḥ

By sacrifice, the Gods gave birth to sacrifice, and the first principles of eternal Dharma, the Ideals of Perfection, were established. Those who live according to the glorious way, ultimately reach the highest abode where the Gods dwell in that ancient perfection.

- 17 -

अभ्द्यः सम्भृतः पृथिव्यैरसाच्च विश्वकर्मणाः समवर्ततागे ।

तस्य त्वष्टा विदधद्रूपमेति तन्मर्त्यस्य देवत्वमाजानमग्रे ॥

abhdyaḥ sambhṛtaḥ pṛthivyairasācca viśvakarmaṇāḥ samavartatāgre
tasya tvaṣṭā vidādhādrūpāmeti tānmārtyasya devatvamājānamagre

In the beginning, the Doer of All distinguished the earth from the waters. Then the Creator gave the knowledge to distinguish the mortal world of humans from the immortal world of the Gods.

\- 18 -

वेदाहमेतं पुरुषं महान्तमादित्यवर्णं तमसः परस्तात् ।

तमेव विदित्वाति मृत्युमेति नान्यः पन्था विद्यतेऽयनाय ॥

vedāhmetaṃ puruṣaṃ mahāntam
ādityavarṇaṃ tamasaḥ parastāt
tameva viditvāti mṛtyumeti
nānyaḥ panthā vidyate-yanāya

I know this full, complete, and perfect consciousness, whose greatness is the color of the sun without darkness. Only those who know this are free from death. There is no other path by which liberation is known.

\- 19 -

प्रजापतिश्चरति गर्भे अन्तरजायमानो बहुधा वि जायते ।

तस्य योनिं परि पश्यन्ति धीरास्

तस्मिन् हतस्थुर्भुवनानि विश्वा ॥

prajāpatiścarati garbhe
antarajāyamāno bahudhā vi jāyate
tasya yoniṃ pari paśyanti dhīrās
tasmin hatasthurbhuvanāni viśvā

The Lord of all Beings Born enters all souls within the womb, and the eternal assumes all forms within the creation. Those who know the Supreme continually look to the divine within, which is established in all existence.

\- 20 -

यो देवेभ्य आतपति यो देवानां पुरोहितः ।

पूर्वो यो देवेभ्यो जातो नमो रुचाय ब्राह्मये ॥

yo devebhya ātapati yo devānāṃ purohitaḥ
pūrvo yo devebhyo jāto namo rucāya brāhmaye

That Supreme Lord illuminates the shining Gods and goes before the Gods in their every endeavor. We continually bow with respect to that illuminated Supreme Divinity, who took birth before the Gods.

- 21 -

रुचं ब्राह्मं जनयन्तो देवा अग्रे तदब्रुवन् ।

यस्त्वैवं ब्रह्मणो विद्यात्तस्य देवा असन् वशे ॥

rucaṃ brāhmaṃ janayanto devā agne tadabruvan
yastvaivaṃ brahmaṇo vidyāttasya devā asan vaśe

Those whose lives are illuminated with the rise of the radiance of divine light joyously proclaim: The Gods are bound to serve those who know the Supreme Divinity in this form, as the one indivisible being.

- 22 -

श्रीश्च ते लक्ष्मीश्च पत्न्यावहोरात्रे पार्श्वे नक्षत्राणि रूपमश्विनौ व्यात्तम् । इष्णन्निषाणामुं म इषाण सर्वलोकं म इषाण ॥

śrīśca te lakṣmīśca patnyāvahorātre pārśve
nakṣatrāṇi rūpamaśvinau vyāttam
iṣṇannişāṇāmuṃ ma iṣāṇa sarvalokaṃ ma iṣāṇa

Oṃ the Highest Respect to you, Goal of all Existence, wife of the full and complete divinity, the night (the Unknowable One), at whose sides are the stars, and who has the form of the relentless search for Truth. Oh Supreme Divinity, Supreme Divinity, my Supreme Divinity, all existence is my Supreme Divinity.

इति द्वितीयोऽध्यायः

iti dvitīyo-dhyāyaḥ

Thus ends the second chapter.

[1] The Puruṣa, the Supreme Being, is the full and complete body of existence. Puru means full, complete, perfect; iṣa means Lord or Ruler, Seer; thus the Seer of Perfection or the Perfect Lord. He requires every function in order to sustain Himself: a Central Nervous System, or Intellect; an Administrative or Defense System, and Circulatory and Nourishments Systems. This makes Him full and complete as an integrated whole. The verse does not mean that children born in a Brahmiṇ family are higher than others, as so often it is interpreted. Rather it shows that the Puruṣa performs every function, and any man wishing perfection, must emulate His perfect nature.

[2] There are many possibilities for the seven limitations defined. The most logical is:

ॐ भूः ॐ भुवः ॐ स्वः ॐ महः ॐ जनः ॐ तपः ॐ सत्यं ।

oṃ bhūḥ oṃ bhuvaḥ oṃ svaḥ oṃ mahaḥ oṃ janaḥ oṃ tapaḥ oṃ satyaṃ

Oṃ Gross Perception; Oṃ Subtle Perception; Oṃ Intuitive Perception; Oṃ the Cosmic Body of Nature; Oṃ the Body of Universal Knowledge; Oṃ the Body of Light; Oṃ the Ultimate Truth, Consciousness, Bliss. Other possibile interpretations are the seven meters, seven levels of heaven and hell, or for that matter all of the various attributes classified by seven.

Chapter 3

हरिः ॐ

hariḥ oṃ
Praise to oṃ

- 1 -

आशुः शिशानो वृषभो न भीमो घनाघनः

क्षोभणश्चर्षणीनाम् ।

संक्रन्दनोऽनिमिष एकवीरः

शतं सेना अजयत् साकमिन्द्रः ॥

āśuḥ śiśāno vṛṣabho na bhīmo ghanāghanaḥ
kṣobhaṇaścarṣaṇīnām
saṃkrandano-nimiṣa ekavīraḥ
śataṃ senā ajayat sākamindraḥ

You move swiftly with your sharp lightning, making our enemies fearful. You are like a bull, slayer of enmity, driver of humanity, extremely radiant, our hero, Indra, who alone conquered a hundred enemy armies.

- 2 -

संक्रन्दनेनानिमिषेण जिष्णुना युत्कारेण

दुश्च्यवनेन धृष्णुना ।

तदिन्द्रेण जयत तत्सहध्वं युधो नर इषुहस्तेन वृष्णा ॥

saṃkrandanenānimiṣeṇa jiṣṇunā yutkāreṇa
duścyavanena dhṛṣṇunā
tadindreṇa jayata tat
sahaḍhvaṃ yudho nara iṣuhastena vṛṣṇā

Oh human warrior, with great words, call for Indra's help. He is radiant, steadfast in victory, unconquerable. He has a luminous light, and an arrow in his hand. He will defeat the armies of your limitations and destroy them.

\- 3 -

स इषुहस्तैः स निषङ्गिभिर्वशी संस्रष्टा स युध इन्द्रोगणेन ।

संसृष्टजित्सोमपा बाहुशर्ध्युग्रधन्वा प्रतिहिताभिरस्ता ॥

sa iṣuhastaiḥ sa niṣaṅgibhirvaśī saṃ sraṣṭā sa yudha indrogaṇena
saṃ sṛṣṭajitsomapā bāhuśarḍhyugradhanvā pratihitābhirastā

Hey warriors, he who controls limitations, who makes war with limitations, who defeats all limitations on the battlefield, who drinks the nectar of devotion, who has great strength in his arms, who is excellent with the bow of determination, who is extremely accurate with his arrows of attention, may that Indra protect us.

\- 4 -

बृहस्पते परि दीया रथेन रक्षोहाऽमित्राँ अपबाधमानः ।

प्रभञ्जन्त्सेनाः प्रमृणो युधा

जयन्नस्माकमेध्यविता रथानाम् ॥

bṛhaspate pari dīyā rathena rakṣohā-mitrāṁ apabādhamānaḥ
prabhañcantsenāḥ pramṛṇo yudhā
jayannasmākameḍhyavitā rathānām

Hey Bṛhaspati, Spirit of the Vast, you destroy all negativity, you destroy all limitations. You are a firm opponent in battle, continually traveling in your chariot. Please protect our conveyance.

\- 5 -

बलविज्ञाय स्थविरः प्रवीरः

सहस्वान् वाजी सहमान उग्रः ।

अभिवीरो अभिसत्त्वा सहोज

जैत्रमिन्द्र रथमा तिष्ठ गोवित् ॥

balavijñāya sthaviraḥ pravīraḥ
sahasvān vājī sahamāna ugraḥ
abhivīro abhisattvā sahoja
jaitramindra rathamā tiṣṭa govit

Hey Indra, Rule of the Pure, you ride on an invincible chariot. You possess divine strength, you exist since ancient times, a strong hero, with much food, above all limitations, fierce in battle. On your four sides are your warriors and the multitude of your helpers. From your strength you reveal divine hymns of knowledge.

- 6 -

गोत्रभिदं गोविदं वज्रबाहुं जयन्तमज्म प्रमृणन्तमोजसा ।
इमं सजाता अनु वीरयध्वमिन्द्रं
सखायो अनु सं रभध्वम् ॥

gotrabhidaṃ govidaṃ vajrabāhuṃ jayantamajma
pramṛṇantamojasā
imaṃ sajātā anu vīrayadhvamindraṃ
sakhāyo anu saṃ rabhadhvam

Hey all you divine beings endowed with equanimity! Invite Indra, the Rule of the Pure, to commence his heroic action. That Indra is well versed in the ways of heroes, well versed in modes of expression, he has arms like a thunderbolt, he is victorious in battle, and he is called Destroyer of Limitations.

- 7 -

अभि गोत्राणि सहसा गाहमानोऽदयो
वीरः शतमन्युरिन्द्रः ।
दुश्च्यवनः पृतनाषाडयुध्योऽस्माकं सेना अवतु प्रयुत्सु ॥

abhi gotrāṇi sahasā gāhamāno-dayo
vīraḥ śatamanyurindraḥ
duśacyavanaḥ pṛtanāṣāḍayudhyo-smākaṃ
senā avatu prayutsu

Indra, Rule of the Pure, protect our armies in battle. Indra, you split apart the cloud which obscures the light of wisdom. You shine with compassion, the hero who performed a hundred sacrifices. You are victorious in all confrontations and superior to every warrior.

- 8 -

इन्द्र आसां नेता बृहस्पतिर्दक्षिणा यज्ञः पुर एतु सोमः ।

देवसेनानामभिभञ्जतीनां जयन्तीनां मरुतो यन्त्वग्रम् ॥

indra āsāṃ netā bṛhaspatir
dakṣiṇā yajñaḥ pura etu somaḥ
devasenānāmabhibhañcatīnāṃ
jayantīnāṃ maruto yantvagram

Let Indra, the Rule of the Pure, be the leader, Bṛhaspati, Spirit of the Vast, be on the right. Let the sacrifice be presided over by Devotion. May the armies of the Gods march on to victory, and may the swiftly proceeding move forward.

- 9 -

इन्द्रस्य वृष्णो वरुणस्य राज्ञ आदित्यानां

मरुतां शर्ध उग्रम् ।

महामनसां भुवनच्यवानां घोषो देवानां जयतामुदस्थात् ॥

indrasya vṛṣṇo varuṇasya rājña ādityānāṃ
marutāṃ śardha ugram
mahāmanasāṃ bhuvanacyavānāṃ
ghoṣo devānāṃ jayatāmudasthāt

Raise your voices in shouts of victory for Indra, who causes the rains of the fulfillment of all desires, for the King Varuṇa, the Lord of Equilibrium, for the twelve Gods, sons of Aditi, the shining ones of non-duality. Praise the swiftly proceeding Gods, all with great minds, the victorious armies who are capable of bringing harmony to the earth.

\- 10 -

उद्धर्षय मघवन्नायुधान्युत्सत्त्वनां मामकानां मनांसि ।

उद्व्रहन् वाजिनां वाजिनान्युद्रथानां जयतां यन्यु घोषाः ॥

uddharṣaya maghavannāyudhānyutsattvanāṃ
māmakānāṃ manāṃ si
udbatrahan vājināṃ
vājinānyudrathānāṃ jayatāṃ yanyu ghoṣāḥ

Oh one of Great Strength, give great bliss to all. Fill our minds with great delight. Oh Slayer of Vṛtra, the changes and modifications of consciousness, come quickly on your invincible chariot with triumphant shouts along with your enthusiastic heroes.

\- 11 -

अस्माकमिन्द्रः समृतेषु ध्वजेष्वस्माकं या इषवस्ता जयन्तु ।

अस्माकं वीरा उत्तरे भवन्त्वस्मां उदेवा अवता हवेषु ॥

asmākamindraḥ samṛteṣu dhvajeṣvasmākaṃ
yā iṣavastā jayantu
asmākaṃ vīrā uttare bhavantvasmāṃ
udevā avatā haveṣu

Oh Indra, Rule of the Pure, topple the flags of all limitations and protect us. May our accurate arrows destroy all enmity. May our multitude of heroic beings receive great delight from the defeat of the armies of limitations. Oh, all you Gods, please protect us.

\- 12 -

अमीषां चित्तं प्रतिलोभयन्ती गृहानाङ्गान्यप्वे परेहि ।

अभि प्रेहि निर्दह हृत्सु

शोकैरन्धेनामित्रास्तमसा सचन्ताम् ॥

amīṣāṃ cittaṃ pratilobhayantī
gṛhānāṅgānyapve parehi
abhi prehi nirdaha hṛtsu
śokairandhenāmitrāstamasā sacantām

Oh Soldiers of Indra's army, if you are tempted by the objects of unfavorable consciousness, then put an end to their manifestations. If you try to accept them, you must go to them. You must see the confusion they bring to your heart and resist union with the intensity of their darkness.

\- 13 -

अवसृष्टा परा पत शरव्ये ब्रह्मसंशिते ।

गच्छामित्रान् प्र पद्यस्व माऽमीषां कं चनोच्छिषः ॥

avasṛṣṭā parā pata śaravye brahmasaṃśite
gacchāmitrān pra padyasva
mā-mīṣāṃ kaṃ canocchiṣaḥ

Oh all divine beings, your sharp weapons bring the armies of limitations low. Enter into the body of five elements and let no enmity remain.

\- 14 -

प्रेता जयता नर इन्द्रो वः शर्म यच्छतु ।

उग्रा वः सन्तु बाहवोऽनाधृष्या यथाऽसथ ॥

pretā jayatā nara indro vaḥ śarma yacchatu
ugrā vaḥ santu bāhavo-nādhṛṣyā yathā-satha

Hey all our multitude of warriors, confront the army of limitations and gain victory. Indra, Rule of the Pure, your victorious form gives great pleasure. Let your arms be strong.

\- 15 -

असौ या सेना मरुतः परेषामभ्यैति न ओजसास्पर्धमाना ।

तां गूहत तमसाऽपव्रतेन यथाऽमी अन्यो अन्यं न जानन् ॥

asau yā senā marutaḥ
pareṣāmabhyaiti na ojasāspardhamānā
tāṃ gūhata tamasā-pavratena
yathā-mī anyo anyaṃ na jānan

Hey Maruts, Lords of Emancipation, let all the enemy warriors who came to battle with us before, dissolve all of their conflicts, so they cannot remember their previous dispositions and all their karmas will be destroyed.

- 16 -

यत्र बाणाः सम्पतन्ति कुमारा विशिखा इव ।

तन्न इन्द्रो बृहस्पतिरदितिः शर्म यच्छतु

विश्वाहा शर्म यच्छतु ॥

yatra bāṇāḥ sampatanti kumārā viśikhā iva
tanna indro bṛhaspatiraditiḥ śarma yacchatu
viśvāhā śarma yacchatu

May the armies of limitations be defeated by the multitude of our warriors' arrows. Thereafter Indra, Bṛhaspati, and the Mother of the Gods, Aditi, will always give us delight.

- 17 -

मर्माणि ते वर्मणा छादयामि

सोमस्त्वा राजाऽमृतेनानुवस्ताम् ।

उरोर्वरीयोवरुणस्ते कृणोतु जयन्तं त्वाऽनु देवा मदन्तु ॥

marmāṇi te varmaṇā chādayāmi
somastvā rājā-mṛtenānuvastām
urorvarīyovaruṇaste kṛṇotu
jayantaṃ tvā-nu devā madantu

Oh you who make sacrifice, we make the armor on your chest impenetrable. May the King of Devotion grant you armor which repels death and makes you invincible. May Varuṇa, the Lord of Equilibrium, make your armor extensive, and may all the Gods be with you and continually inspire you with enthusiasm.

इति तृतीयोऽध्यायः

iti tṛtīyo-dhyāyaḥ

Thus ends the third chapter.

Chapter 4

हरिः ॐ

hariḥ oṃ

Praise to oṃ

\- 1 -

विभ्राड् बृहत्पिबतु सोम्यं मध्वायुर्दधद्यज्ञपतावविहुतम ।

वातजूतो यो अभिरक्षतित्मना प्रजाः

पुपोष पुरुधा वि राजति ॥

vibhrād bṛhātpibatu somyaṃ
madhvāyurdadhadyajñapatāvavi hutam
vātajūto yo abhirakṣatitmanā prajāḥ
pupoṣa purudhā vi rājāti

We offer this sweet libation of the nectar of immortal devotion to the Lord of the Vast, the Light of Wisdom, to drink. He inspires the Lord of Emancipation, and protects and nourishes all the children of the kingdom which He rules.

\- 2 -

उदुत्यं जातवेदसं देवं वहन्ति केतवः ।

दृशे विश्वाय सूर्यम् ॥

udutyaṃ jātvedasaṃ devaṃ vahānti ketavaḥ
dṛśe viśvāya sūryam

The Sun is the Light of Wisdom, knower of all, omnipresent, the God who illuminates all the universe with perception.

\- 3 -

येना पावक चक्षसा भुरण्यन्तं जनाँ२ अनु ।

त्वं वरुण पश्यसि ॥

yenā pāvaka cakṣasā bhuraṇyantaṃ janām̐ anu
tvaṃ varuṇa paśyāsi

With the same perception of a Guardian King, looking at his people, oh Lord of Equilibrium, with that same perception look at us.

- 4 -

देव्यावध्वर्यू आ गतं रथेन सूर्यत्वचा ।

मध्वा यज्ञं समञ्जाथे ।

तं प्रक्नथाऽयं वेनश्चित्रं देवानाम् ॥

devyāvadhvaryū ā gataṃ rathena sūryatvacā
madhvā yajñaṃ samañcāthe
taṃ praknathā-yaṃ venaścitraṃ devānām

Hey divine priests of the Yajur Veda, Aśvins. Come to the sacrifice on your chariots as bright as the sun and accept our offerings moistened with honey. Among the Gods you are extremely ancient. May humanity gain your wisdom.

- 5 -

तं प्रक्नथा पूर्वथा विश्वथेमथा ज्येष्ठतातिं बर्हिषदँ स्वर्विदम् ।

प्रतीचीनं वृजनं दोहसे धुनिमाशुं जयन्तमनु यासु वर्धसे ॥

taṃ praknathā pūrvathā viśvathemathā jyeṣṭhatātiṃ barhiṣadam̐ svarvidam
pratīcīnaṃ vṛjanaṃ dohase dhunimāśuṃ jayantamanu yāsu vardhase

Oh Lord, we are offering you the nectar of our devotion in the sacrificial fire, just like the ancient sages and seers of antiquity. Give us the fruit of our sacrificial offering, just as you gave to them. We are singing your praises so that you will remove from us all obstacles, as you did for those of ancient times.

- 6 -

अयं वेनश्चोदयत्पृश्निगर्भा ज्योतिर्जरायू रजसो विमाने ।

इममपां सङ्गमे सूर्यस्य शिशुं न विप्रा मतिभीरिहन्ति ॥

ayaṃ venaścodayatpṛśnigarbhā jyotir
jarāyū rajaso vimāne
imamapāṃ saṅgame sūryasya
śiśuṃ na viprā matibhīrihanti

Oh Lord, you inspire the creation with the rise of your light, radiating from various conveyances. We see the lightning of illumination, the Moon of Devotion, the Light of Wisdom, illuminating existence in union with you, just like a young student with his teacher.

\- 7 -

चित्रं देवानामुदगादनीकं चक्षुर्मित्रस्य वरुणस्याग्नेः ।

आप्रा द्यावापृथिवी अन्तरिक्षं

सूर्य आत्मा जगतस्तस्थुषश्च ॥

citraṃ devānāmudagādanīkaṃ
cakṣurmitrasya varuṇasyāgneḥ
āprā dyāvāpṛthivī antarikṣaṃ
sūrya ātmā jagatastasthuṣaśca

Oh Light of Wisdom, established as the soul of all perceivable existence, you dwell above the earth, the atmosphere, and the heavens in various forms of divinity, as the eyes of Friendship, the Lord of Equilibrium, and the Fire of Purification.

\- 8 -

आन इडाभिर्विदथे सुशस्ति विश्वानरः सविता देव एतु ।

अपि यथा युवानो मत्सथा नो विश्वं

जगदभिपित्वे मनीषा ॥

āna idābhirvidathe suśasti
viśvānaraḥ savitā deva etu
api yathā yuvāno matsathā no viśvaṃ
jagadabhipitve manīṣā

Oh, God Savitur, light of the heavens, who brings welfare to the Universe, come, full of our praises, into the Iḍa. Enter into the house of sacrifice. Hey oldest of the Gods, in the same form as you delight me when you come, in that same form delight the entire perceivable universe by giving us pure knowledge.

- 9 -

यदद्य कच्च वृत्रहन्नुदगा अभि सूर्य ।

सर्वं तदिन्द्र ते वशे ॥

yadadya kacca vṛtrahannudagā abhi sūrya
sarvaṃ tadindra te vaśe

Oh, eternal Sun, the Light of Wisdom who destroys all darkness, today wherever you may rise, bring all under your control, because you are the controller of all.

- 10 -

तरणिर्विश्वदर्शतो ज्योतिष्कृदसि सूर्य ।

विश्वमा भासि रोचनम् ॥

tarāṇarviśvadarśato jyotiṣkṛdasi sūrya
viṣvamā bhāsi rocanam

Hey Sun, you are the Illuminator of the Light of the universe. The universe is illuminated in your light. You traverse the heavens and make the universe perceivable.

- 11 -

तत्सूर्यस्य देवत्वं तन्महित्वं मध्या कर्तोर्विततं सं जभार ।

यदेदयुक्त हरितः सधस्थादाद्रात्री वासस्तनुते सिमस्मै ॥

tatsūryasya devatvaṃ tanmahitvaṃ madhyā
kartorvitataṃ saṃ jabhāra
yadedayukta haritaḥ sadhasthādādrātrī
vāsastanute simasmai

Oh, God Sun, you have such greatness and authority that you can withdraw your light even in the midst of the world's activity. When your golden orb sets into the horizon, then all creation is thrust into darkness.

- 12 -

तन्मित्रस्य वरुणस्याभिचक्षे सूर्यो रूपं कृणुते द्योरुपस्थे ।

अनन्तमन्यद्रुशदस्य पाजः कृष्णमन्यद्धरितः सं भरन्ति ॥

tānmitrasya varuṇasyābhicakṣe
sūryo rūpaṃ kṛṇute dyorupasthe
anantamanyadruśadasya pājaḥ
kṛṣṇamanyaddharitaḥ saṃ bharanti

Oh, Sun, you are the light in the eyes of Mitra and Varuṇa and illuminate all the activities of heaven. Sometimes you are seen illuminating the infinite. Sometimes you are seen covering all existence with darkness.

- 13 -

बण्महाँ२ असि सूर्य बडादित्य महाँ२ असि ।

महस्ते सतो महिमा पनस्यतेऽद्धा देव महाँ२ असि ॥

baṇmahām̐asi sūrya badāditya mahām̐ asi
mahaste sato mahimā panasyate
-ddhā deva mahām̐ asi

Oh, Sun, you are great! Oh omnipresent, one without a second, you are great! In truth, you are great! All the worlds proclaim your glory! You are great indeed!

- 14 -

बट् सूर्य श्रवसा महाँ२ असि सत्रा देव महाँ२ असि ।

मह्ना देवानामसुर्यः पुरोहितो विभु ज्योतिरदाभ्यम् ॥

baṭ sūrya śravasā mahām̐ asi satrā deva mahām̐ asi
mahnā devānāmasuryaḥ
purohito vibhu jyotiradābhyam

Oh Sun, yours is the true wealth! You are great! Yours is the true fame! You are great! Oh God, your greatness is most excellent among the Gods! You make the sacred offering of light to all creation.

\- 15 -

श्रायन्त इव सूर्यं विश्वेदिन्द्रस्य भक्षत ।

वसूनि जाते जनमान ओजसा प्रति भागं न दीधिम ॥

śrāyanta iva sūryaṃ viśvedindrasya bhakṣata
vasūni jāte janamāna ojasā
prati bhāgaṃ na dīdhima

Because of the sun, Indra causes the rain to fall, which nourishes all life with food. As children nourished by that food, it is necessary to plant the seeds of that wealth for future generations.

\- 16 -

अद्या देवा उदिता सूर्यस्य निरं हसः पिपृता निरवद्यात् ।

तन्नो मित्रो वरुणो मामहन्तामदितिः सिन्धुः

पृथिवी उत द्यौः ॥

adyā devā uditā sūryasya niraṃ
hasaḥ pipṛtā niravadyāt
tanno mitro varuṇo māmahantām
aditiḥ sindhuḥ pṛthivī uta dyauḥ

Hey all Gods, turn us away from sin, remove all confusion, all evil. May today's sunrise make us pure. May Mitra, Varuṇa, Mother of the Gods, Aditi, rivers, earth and heaven help us to fulfill our promise.

\- 17 -

आ कृष्णेन रजसा वर्तमनो निवेशयन्नमृतं मर्त्यं च ।

हिरण्ययेन सविता रथेना देवो याति भुवनानि पश्यन् ॥

ā kṛṣṇena rajasā vartamano
niveśayannamṛtaṃ martyaṃ ca
hiraṇyayena savitā rathenā
devo yāti bhuvanāni paśyan

The Golden Orb mounted on his chariot, the God who shines with wisdom, traverses the universe bringing light and then darkness, distinguishing the divine from the mortal. He is the God who perceives all existence.

इति चतुर्थोऽध्यायः

iti caturtho-dhyāyaḥ

Thus ends the fourth chapter.

Chapter 5

हरिः ॐ

hariḥ oṃ

Praise to oṃ

- 1 -

नमस्ते रुद्र मन्यव उतो त इषवे नमः ।

बाहुभ्यामुत ते नमः ॥

namaste rudra manyava uto ta iṣave namaḥ
bāhubhyāmuta te namaḥ

I bow to you, Rudra, Reliever of Sufferings, who gives wisdom to all. I bow to your anger that purifies iniquity. I bow to the strength of your arms.

- 2 -

या ते रुद्र शिवा तनूरघोराऽपापकाशिनी ।

तया नस्तन्वा सन्तमया गिरिशन्ताभि चाकशीहि ॥

yā te rudra śivā tanūraghorā-pāpakāśinī
tayā nastanvā santamayā girisantābhi cākaśīhi

Hey Rudra, Reliever of Sufferings, along with the Divine Mother, your beautiful body grants welfare and merit upon seeing it. Hey Lord of Mountains, please look in our direction with that pleasing countenance.

- 3 -

यामिषुं गिरिशन्त हस्ते बिभर्ष्यस्तवे ।

शिवां गिरित्र तां कुरु मा हिंसीः पुरुषं जगत् ॥

yāmiṣuṃ giriśanta haste bibharṣyastave
śivāṃ giritra tāṃ kuru mā hiṃ siḥ puruṣaṃ jagat

Hey Lord of Mountains, because our enemies are most formidable, you hold a bow in your hands. Oh you into whom all life dissolves, give welfare. Do not allow violence to mankind or the world.

- 4 -

शिवेन वचसात्त्वा गिरिशाच्छा वदामसि ।

यथा नः सर्वमिज्जगदयक्ष्मं सुमना असत् ॥

śivena vacasāttvā giriśācchā vadāmasi
yathā naḥ sarvamijjagadayakṣmaṃ sumanā asat

Oh Lord of the Mountains, we are singing this meritorious song of praise to you, and bowing with pure devotion, praying that you make the world free from disease.

- 5 -

अध्यवोचदधिवक्ता प्रथमो दैव्यो भिषक् ।

अहींश्च सर्वाञ्जम्भयन्त्सर्वाश्च

यातुधान्योऽधराचीः परा सुव ॥

adhyavocadadhivāktā prathamo daivyo bhiṣak
ahīṃśca sarvāñjambhayantsarvāśca
yātudhānyo-dharācīḥ parā suva

Oh you who have many faces, you are worthy of being worshipped and remembered with my greatest strength of effort, because you are the divine physician. Hey Rudra, Reliever of Sufferings, destroy all poisons and all demonical maladies of the body and mind.

- 6 -

असौ यस्ताम्रो अरुण उत बभ्रुः सुमङ्गलः ।

ये चैनं रुद्रा अभितो दिक्षु श्रिताः

सहस्रशो वैषां हेडऽ ईमहे ॥

asau yastāmro aruṇa uta babhruḥ sumaṅgalaḥ
ye cai naṃ rudrā abhito dikṣu śritāḥ
sahasraśo vaiṣāṃ heḍa-imahe

His form is bright when he rises, and at the end of the day red. At other times it is yellow. Oh manifestation of welfare, whose thousand rays take refuge in the East, we dissolve his anger in our devotion.

\- 7 -

असौ योऽवसर्पति नीलग्रीवो विलोहितः ।

उतैनं गोपा अदृश्रन्नदृन्नुदहार्यः स दृष्टो मृडयाति नः ॥

asau yo-vasarpati nīlagrīvo vilohitaḥ
utainaṃ gopā adṛśrannadṛśrannudahāryaḥ
sa dṛṣto mṛḍayāti naḥ

He is the form of the one eternal light in constant movement, who the protectors of light and the waters of truth always long to see. May he give us the delight of his perception.

\- 8 -

नमोऽस्तु नीलग्रीवाय सहस्राक्षाय मीढुषे ।

अथो ये अस्य सत्त्वानोऽहं तेभ्योऽकरं नमः ॥

namo-stu nīlgrīvāya sahasrākṣāya mīḍhuṣe
atho ye asya sattvāno-haṃ tebhyo-karaṃ namaḥ

I bow to he who is everywhere, who sees all, who has a blue throat. To he who is completely full, I bow.

\- 9 -

प्रमुञ्च धन्वनस्त्वमुभयोरार्त्न्योर्ज्याम् ।

याश्च ते हस्त इषवः परा ता भगवो वप ॥

pramuñca dhanvanastvamubhayorārtnyorjyām
yāśca te hasta iṣavaḥ parā tā bhagavo vapa

Oh Lord, open the enemy's bow string from its two sides and let the arrows fall from his hands to the ground.

\- 10 -

विज्यं दनुः कपर्दिनो विशल्यो बाणवां२ उत ।

अनेशन्नस्य या इषव आभुरस्य निषङ्गधिः ॥

vijyaṃ danuḥ kapardino viśalyo bāṇavāṃ uta
aneśannasya yā iṣava ābhurasya niṣaṅgadhiḥ

Oh Rudra, Reliever of Sufferings, with matted hair, let his

bow be without a bow string. Let his arrows be without arrowheads, let his arrow holder be empty.

\- 11 -

या ते हेतिर्मीढुष्टम हस्ते बभूव ते धनुः ।

तयाऽस्मान्विश्वतस्त्वमयक्ष्मया परि भुज ॥

yā te hetirmīḍhuṣtama haste babhūva te dhanuḥ
tayā-smānviśvatastvamayakṣmayā pari bhuja

Oh Grantor of desires, with a bow in your hand, protect us on every side from all kinds of conflict.

\- 12 -

परि ते धन्वनो हेतिरस्मान्वृणक्तु विश्वतः ।

अथो य इषुधिस्तवारे अस्मन्नि धेहि तम् ॥

pari te dhanvano hetirasmānvṛṇaktuviśvataḥ
atho ya iṣudhistavāre asmanni dhehi tam

Hey Rudra, Reliever of Sufferings, your bow and arrows are for the purpose of maintaining peace. May we renounce our selfish attachment for your peace.

\- 13 -

अवतत्य धनुष्ट्वं सहस्राक्ष शतेषुधे ।

निशीर्य शल्यानां मुखा शिवो नः सुमना भव ॥

avatatya dhanuṣtvaṃ sahasrākṣa śateṣudhe
niśīrya śalyānāṃ mukhā śivo naḥ sumanā bhava

Oh Rudra, Reliever of Sufferings, who sees with a thousand eyes. With hundreds of weapons, with bows and arrows, and all manner of weapons, may you bless us with consciousness filled with peace and beauty.

\- 14 -

नमस्त आयुधायानातताय धृष्णवे ।

उभाभ्यामुत ते नमो बाहुभ्यान्तव धन्वने ॥

namasta āyudhāyānātatāya dhṛṣṇave
ubhābhyāmuta te namo bāhubhyāntava dhanvane

Oh Rudra, Reliever of Sufferings, we bow to your weapons. We bow to your bow and arrows and to your two strong arms. We bow and we bow.

- 15 -

मा नो महान्तमुत मा नो अर्भकं मा न

उक्षन्तमुत मा न उक्षितम् ।

मा नो वधीः पितरं मोत मातरं

मा नः प्रियास्तन्वो रुद्र रीरिषः ॥

mā no mahāntamuta mā no arabhakaṃ mā na
ukṣantamuta mā na ukṣitam
mā no vidhīḥ pitaraṃ mota mātraṃ
mā naḥ priyāstanvo rudra rīriṣaḥ

Oh Rudra, Reliever of Sufferings, do not judge the great among us. Do not judge the elderly, nor the children, nor the youth. Do not judge the children in the womb, nor our fathers or mothers or our beloveds.

- 16 -

मा नस्तोके तनये मा न आयुषि मा नो

गोषु मा नो अश्वेषु रीरिषः ।

मा नो वीरान् रुद्र भामिनो वधीर्हविष्मन्तः

सदमित्त्वा हवामहे ॥

mā nastoke tanaye mā na āyuṣi mā no
goṣu mā no aśveṣu rīriṣaḥ
mā no vīrān rudra bhāmino vadhīrhaviṣmantaḥ
sadamittvā havāmahe

Oh Rudra, Reliever of Sufferings, do not judge our children or grandchildren, our lives, or cows or horses. With offerings of oblations we propitiate you in the sacred fire sacrifice.

- 17 -

नमो हिरण्यबाहवे सेनान्ये दिशां च पतये नमः ॥

namo hiraṇyaṇabāhave senānye diśāṃ ca pataye namaḥ

We bow to the one with golden arms and to he who has a vast army and to the lord of the directions

- 18 -

नमो वृक्षेभ्यो हरिकेशेभ्यः पशूनां पतये नमः ॥

namo vṛkṣebhyo harikeśebhyaḥ paśūnāṃ pataye namaḥ

We bow to the trees with golden leaves and to the lord of all animals

- 19 -

नमः शष्पिञ्जराय त्विषीमते पथीनां पतये नमः ॥

namaḥ śiṣpiñjarāya tviṣīmate pathīnāṃ pataye namaḥ

We bow to he who is extremely beautiful and of yellow and red hue and to he who protects the paths

- 20 -

नमो हरिकेशायोपवीतिने पुष्टानां पतये नमः ॥

namo hari keśāyopavītine puṣṭānāṃ pataye namaḥ

We bow to he who has golden hair and wears a sacred thread and to he who is the lord of all nourishment

- 21 -

नमो बभ्लुषाय व्याधिनेऽन्नानां पतये नमः ॥

namo babhluṣāya vyādine-nnānāṃ pataye namaḥ

We bow to he who rides on a bull and destroys enemies and to the lord of food

- 22 -

नमो भवस्य हेत्यै जगतां पतये नमः ॥

namo bhavasya hetyai jagatāṃ pataye namaḥ

We bow to he who dissolves the world of objects and relationships and to the protector of the perceivable world

- 23 -

नमो रुद्रायाततायिने क्षेत्राणां पतये नमः ॥

namo rudrāyātatāyine kṣetrāṇāṃ pataye namaḥ

We bow to he who is prepared for war and to the protector of the body

- 24 -

नमः सूतायाहन्त्यै वनानां पतये नमः ॥

namaḥ sūtāyāhantyai vanānāṃ pataye namaḥ

We bow to the charioteer of creation and to the lord of forests

- 25 -

नमो रोहिताय स्थपतये वृक्षाणां पतये नमः ॥

namo rohitāya sthapataye vṛkṣāṇāṃ pataye namaḥ

We bow to he who is established as the lord of light and to the lord of trees

- 26 -

नमो भुवन्तये वारिवस्कृतायौषधीनां पतये नमः ॥

namo bhuvantaye vārivaskṛtāyauṣadhīnāṃ pataye namaḥ

We bow to he who is the extension of the entire earth and to the giver of wealth and to the lord of all vegetation

- 27 -

नमो मन्त्रिणे वाणिजाय कक्षाणां पतये नमः ॥

namo mantriṇe vāṇījāya kakṣāṇāṃ pataye namaḥ

We bow to the lord of all victorious vibrations in mantras and to the lord of those who make a loud battle cry

- 28 -

नम उच्चैर्घोषायाक्रन्दयते पत्तीनां पतये नमः ॥

nama ucairghoṣāyākrandayate pattīnāṃ pataye namaḥ

We bow to he whose arrows move swiftly from the bow in battle and to the protector of those who take refuge

- 29 -

नमः कृत्स्नाय तया धावते सत्त्वनाम पतये नमः ॥

namaḥ kṛtsnāya tayā dhāvate sattvanāma pataye namaḥ

We bow to he who is the entire whole in completeness and to he who is the lord of all living beings

- 30 -

नमः सहमानाय निव्याधिन आव्याधिनीनां पतये नमः ॥

namaḥ sahamānāya nivyādhina āvyadhinīnāṃ pataye namaḥ

We bow to he who is with all thoughts and to he who is free from all illness and the lord of the wounded

- 31 -

नमो निषङ्गिणे ककुभाय स्तेनानां पतये नमः ॥

namo niṣaṅgiṇe kakubhāya stenānāṃ pataye namaḥ

We bow to he who is the lord who sits upon the summit and who disciplines thieves

- 32 -

नमो निचेरवे परिचरायारण्यानां पतये नमः ॥

namo nicerave paricarāyāraṇyānāṃ pataye namaḥ

We bow to he who is the lord of those who behave respectfully and to the Supreme Lord of all who move in the forest

- 33 -

नमो वञ्चते परिवञ्चते स्तायूनां पतये नमः ॥

namo vañcate parivañcate stāyūnāṃ pataye namaḥ

We bow to he who moves secretly and who moves in supreme secrecy

- 34 -

नमो निषङ्गिण इषुधिमते तस्कराणां पतये नमः ॥

namo niṣaṅgiṇa iṣudhimate taskarāṇāṃ pataye namaḥ

We bow to he who holds a quiver full of arrows and who is in constant jāpa

- 35 -

नमः सृकायिभ्यो जिघांसद्भ्यो मुष्णतां पतये नमः ॥

namaḥ sṛkāyibhyo jighāṃ sadbhyo muṣṇatāṃ pataye namaḥ

We bow to he who holds a thunderbolt and who protects the wealth of the land

- 36 -

नमोऽसिमद्भ्यो नक्तञ्चरद्भ्यो विकृन्तानां पतये नमः

namo-simadbhyo naktañcaradbhyo vikṛantānāṃ pataye namaḥ

We bow to he who moves in the night and who causes all transformation

- 37 -

नम उष्णीषिणे गिरिचराय कुलुञ्चानां पतये नमः ॥

nama uṣṇīṣiṇe giricarāya kuluñcānāṃ pataye namaḥ

We bow to he who wears a turban for a crown and who is lord of the houses in the land

- 38 -

नम इषुमद्भ्यो धन्वायिभ्यश्च वो नमः ॥

nama iṣumadbhyo dhanvāyibhyaśca vo namaḥ

We bow to he who is the great desire or target and who lifts the bow

- 39 -

नम आतन्वानेभ्यो प्रतिदधानेभ्यश्च वो नमः ॥

nama ātanvānebhyo pratidadhānebhyaśca vo namaḥ

We bow to he who mounts the arrow into the bow and who adjusts the arrow in the bow

- 40 -

नम आयच्छद्भ्योऽस्यद्भ्यश्च वो नमः ॥

nama āyacchadbhyo-syadbhyaśca vo namaḥ

We bow to he who stretches the bow string and who is the abode of power

- 41 -

नमो विसृजद्भ्यो विध्यद्भ्यश्च वो नमः ॥

namo visṛjadbhyo vidhyadbhyaśca vo namaḥ

We bow to he who takes careful aim and to he who worships and honors the divine and offers his success

- 42 -

नमः स्वपद्भ्यो जाग्रद्भ्यश्च वो नमः ॥

namaḥ svapadbhyo jāgradbhyaśca vo namaḥ

We bow to he who is felt in dreaming and waking consciousness

- 43 -

नमः शयानेभ्य आसीनेभ्यश्च वो नमः ॥

namaḥ śayānebhya āsīnebhyaśca vo namaḥ

We bow to he who is still and he who moves

- 44 -

नमस्तिष्ठद्भ्यो धावद्भ्यश्चवो नमः ॥

namastiṣṭadbhyo dhāvadbhyaścavo namaḥ

We bow to he who is established and he who advances

- 45 -

नमः सभाभ्यः सभापतिभ्यश्च वो नमः ॥

namaḥ sabhābhyaḥ sabhāpatibhyaśca vo namaḥ

We bow to he who is present in the community and is lord of the multitudes

- 46 -

नमोऽश्वेभ्योऽश्वपतिभ्यश्च वो नमः ॥

namo-śvebhyo-śvapatibhyaśca vo namaḥ

We bow to he who is the horse and the lord of horses

- 47 -

नम आव्याधिनीभ्यो विविध्यन्तीभ्यश्च वो नमः ॥

nama āvyādhinībhyo vividhyadhantībhyaśca vo namaḥ

We bow to he who is always the same and who is hidden as the divinity within all the various forms

- 48 -

नम उगणाभ्यस्तृंहतीभ्यश्च वो नमः ॥

nama ugaṇābhyastṛṃ hatībhyaśca vo namaḥ

We bow to he whose extensive army slays all difficulties and adversities

- 49 -

नमो गणेभ्यो गणपतिभ्यश्च वो नमः ॥

namo gaṇebhyo ganapatibhyaśca vo namaḥ

We bow to he who is the multitude and the lord of the multitudes

- 50 -

नमो व्रातेभ्यो व्रातपतिभ्यश्च वो नमः ॥

namo vrātebhyo vrātapatibhyaśca vo namaḥ

We bow to he who is the vow of worship and the lord of the vow

- 51 -

नमो गृत्सेभ्यो गृत्सपतिभ्यश्च वो नमः ॥

namo gṛtsebhyo gṛtsapatibhyaśca vo namaḥ

We bow to he who is the illumination of love and lord of the illumination

- 52 -

नमो विरूपेभ्यो विश्वरूपेभ्यश्च वो नमः ॥

namo virūpebhyo viśvarūpebhyaśca vo namaḥ

We bow to he who is without form and is the form of the universe

- 53 -

नमः सेनाभ्यः सेनानिभ्यश्च वो नमः ॥

namaḥ senābhyaḥ senānibhyaśca vo namaḥ

We bow to he who is the army and the lord of the army

- 54 -

नमो रथिभ्यो अरथेभ्यश्च वो नमः ॥

namo rathibhyo arathebhyaśca vo namaḥ

We bow to he who is upon a chariot and without a chariot

- 55 -

नमः क्षतृभ्यः संग्रहीतृभ्यश्च वो नमः ॥

namaḥ kṣatṛbhyaḥ saṃgrahītṛbhyaśca vo namaḥ

We bow to he who has dominion and who holds together all existence

- 56 -

नमो महद्भ्यो अर्भकेभ्यश्च वो नमः ॥

namo mahadbhyo arbhakebhyaśca vo namaḥ

We bow to he who is the great and who is the small

- 57 -

नमस्तक्षभ्यो रथकारेभ्यश्च वो नमः ॥

namastakṣabhyo rathakārebhyaśca vo namaḥ

We bow to he who is the creator and the protector

- 58 -

नमः कुलालेभ्यः कर्मारेभ्यश्च वो नमः ॥

namaḥ kulālebhyaḥ karmarebhyaśca vo namaḥ

We bow to he who works with clay and he who works with iron

- 59 -

नमो निषादेभ्यः पुञ्जिष्ठेभ्यश्च वो नमः ॥

namo niṣādebhyaḥ puñciṣtebhyaśca vo namaḥ

We bow to he who is seated in an āsana and who is established within the multitudes

- 60 -

नमः श्वनिभ्यो मृगयुभ्यश्च वो नमः ॥

namaḥ śvanibhyo mṛgayubhyaśca vo namaḥ

We bow to he who is with the lowly and is with those who seek

- 61 -

नमः श्वभ्यः श्वपतिभ्यश्च वो नमः ॥

namaḥ śvabhyaḥ śvapatibhyaśca vo namaḥ

We bow to he who is with those who are in misery and to the lord of the miserable

- 62 -

नमो भवाय च रुद्राय च ॥

namo bhavāya ca rudrāya ca

We bow to he who is all existence and to the Reliever of Sufferings

- 63 -

नमः शर्वाय च पशुपतये च ॥

namaḥ śarvaya ca paśupataye ca

We bow to he who destroys all enmity and to the lord of animals

- 64 -

नमो नीलग्रीवाय च शितिकण्ठाय च ॥

namo nīlagrīvāya ca śitikaṇṭhāya ca

We bow to he who has a blue neck and who has a dark blue throat

- 65 -

नमः कपर्दिने च व्युप्तकेशाय च ॥

namaḥ kapardine ca vyuptakeśāya ca

We bow to he whose hair is tangled and whose hair is disheveled

- 66 -

नमः सहस्राक्षाय च शतधन्वने च ॥

namaḥ sahasrākṣāya ca śatadhanvane ca

We bow to he who has a thousand eyes and who is seen in a hundred rainbows

- 67 -

नमो गिरिशयाय च शिपिविष्टाय च ॥

namo giriśayāya ca śipiviṣṭāya ca

We bow to he who rests in the mountains and who is established in rays of light

- 68 -

नमो मीढुष्टमाय चेषुमते च ॥

namo mīḍhuṣṭamāya ceṣumate ca

We bow to he who gives bountifully and to he who is with those who endeavor to reach the goal

- 69 -

नमो ह्रस्वाय च वामनाय च ॥

namo hrasvāya ca vāmanāya ca

We bow to he who is with those who are short and those who are dwarfed

- 70 -

नमो बृहते च वर्षीयसे च ॥

namo bṛhate ca varṣiyase ca

We bow to he who is with those who are great and who is with those who pour forth goodness

- 71 -

नमो वृद्धाय च सवृधे च ॥

namo vṛddhāya ca savṛdhe ca

We bow to he who is with those who continue to grow and who is with those who inspire growth

- 72 -

नमोऽग्याय च प्रथमाय च ॥

namo-gyāya ca prathamāya ca

We bow to he who is with those who take the lead and who is with those who are foremost

- 73 -

नम आशवे चाजिराय च ॥

nama āśave cājirāya ca

We bow to he who acts quickly and who excels

- 74 -

नमः शीघ्र्याय च शीभ्याय च ॥

namaḥ śīghryāya ca śībhyāya ca

We bow to he who is fast and he who moves with speed

- 75 -

नम ऊर्म्याय चास्वण्याय च ॥

nama ūrmyāya cāsvaṇyāya ca

We bow to he who has become manifest and who inhabits within his manifestation

- 76 -

नमो नादेयाय च द्वीप्याय च ॥

namo nādeyāya ca dvīpyāya ca

We bow to he who flows like a river and who inhabits the islands

- 77 -

नमो ज्येष्ठाय च कनिष्ठाय च ॥

namo jyeṣṭāya ca kaniṣṭāya ca

We bow to he who is oldest and he who is youngest

- 78 -

नमः पूर्वजाय चापरजाय च ॥

namaḥ pūrvajāya cāparajāya ca

We bow to he who was the first born and who will be the last to be born

- 79 -

नमो मध्यमाय चापगल्भाय च ॥

namo madhyamāya cāpagalbhāya ca

We bow to he who will be born in the middle and to he who is not perplexed

- 80 -

नमो जघन्याय च बुध्न्याय च ॥

namo jaghanyāya ca budhnyāya ca

We bow to he who is with the least important and to he who is with the intelligent

- 81 -

नमः सोभ्याय च प्रतिसर्याय च ॥

namaḥ sobhyāya ca pratisaryāya ca

We bow to he who is pure and who is the supreme lord of rivers

- 82 -

नमो याम्याय च क्षेम्याय च ॥

namo yāmyāya ca kṣemyāya ca

We bow to he who controls and who abides in tranquility

- 83 -

नमः श्लोक्याय चावसान्याय च ॥

namaḥ ślokyāya cāvasānyāya ca

We bow to he who is expressed in verse and who is the redeemer of the distressed

- 84 -

नम उर्वर्याय च खल्याय च ॥

nama urvaryāya ca khalyāya ca

We bow to he who makes the soil fertile and who fills the granary

- 85 -

नमो वन्याय च कक्ष्याय च ॥

namo vanyāya ca kakṣyāya ca

We bow to he who dwells in the forests and who dwells in the grass

- 86 -

नमः श्रवाय च प्रतिश्रवाय च ॥

namaḥ śravāya ca pratiśravāya ca

We bow to he who is celebrated with praise and who is celebrated with supreme praise

- 87 -

नम आशुषेणाय चाशुरथाय च ॥

nama āśuṣeṇāya cāśurathāya ca

We bow to he who is with those who move quickly and with those who moves on the fastest conveyance

- 88 -

नमः शूराय चावभेदिने च ॥

namaḥ śūrāya cāvabhedine ca

We bow to he who is mighty and who allows no division

- 89 -

नमो बिल्मिने च कवचिने च ॥

namo bilmine ca kavacine ca

We bow to he who wears a head covering and who wears armor

- 90 -

नमो वर्मिणे च वरूथिने च ॥

namo varmiṇe ca varūthine ca

We bow to he who wears protective mail and who wears various protection

- 91 -

नमः श्रुताय च श्रुतसेनाय च ॥

namaḥ śrutāya ca śrutasenāya ca

We bow to he whose fame is celebrated and whose army's fame is celebrated

- 92 -

नमो दुन्दुभ्याय चाहनन्याय च ॥

namo dundubhyāya cāhananyāya ca

We bow to he who beats the drum and who is bold and courageous

- 93 -

नमो धृष्णवे च प्रमृशाय च ॥

namo dhṛṣṇave ca pramṛśāya ca

We bow to he who is considerate and who is in constant jāpa

- 94 -

नमो निषङ्गिणे चेषुधिमते च ॥

namo niṣaṅgiṇe ceṣudhimate ca

We bow to he who is sought after and who is sharply focused

- 95 -

नमस्तीक्ष्णेषवे चायुधिने च ॥

namastīkṣṇeṣave cāyudhine ca

We bow to he who has sharp weapons and who is beyond all war

- 96 -

नमः स्वायुधाय च सुधन्वने च ॥

namaḥ svāyudhāya ca sudhanvane ca

We bow to he who has no enmity and who has an excellent bow

- 97 -

नमः स्रुत्याय च पथ्याय च ॥

namaḥ srutyāya ca pathyāya ca

We bow to he who is heard of in the Vedas and who is the path

- 98 -

नमः काट्याय च नीप्याय च ॥

namaḥ kāṭyāya ca nīpyāya ca

We bow to he who is unfathomably deep and who is at the foot of the mountain

- 99 -

नमः कुल्याय च सरस्याय च ॥

namaḥ kulyāya ca sarasyāya ca

We bow to he who is a stream and he who is an ocean

- 100 -

नमो नादेयाय च वैशन्ताय च ॥

namo nādeyāya ca vaiśantāya ca

We bow to he who is a river and he who is a tank

- 101 -

नमः कूप्याय चावट्याय च ॥

namaḥ kūpyāya cāvaṭyāya ca

We bow to he who is a well and he who is invoked by others

- 102 -

नमो वीध्र्याय चातप्याय च ॥

namo vīdhryāya cātapyāya ca

We bow to he who is worshipped and he who is the object of purifying austerities

- 103 -

नमो मेघ्याय च विद्युत्याय च ॥

namo meghyāya ca vidyutyāya ca

We bow to he who is the cloud that obscures wisdom and he who is the lightning that shines forth with illumination

- 104 -

नमो वर्ष्याय चावर्ष्याय च ॥

namo varṣyāya cāvarṣyāya ca

We bow to he who is rain and who pours forth the rain

- 105 -

नमो वात्याय च रेष्म्याय च ॥

namo vātyāya ca reṣmyāya ca

We bow to he who moves with the wind and who moves with the storm

- 106 -

नमो वास्तव्याय च वास्तुपाय च ॥

namo vāstavyāya ca vāstupāya ca

We bow to he who is true and genuine and who is the lord of the home

- 107 -

नमः सोमाय च रुद्राय च ॥

namaḥ somāya ca rudrāya ca

We bow to he who is the moon of devotion and who is the Reliever of Suffering

- 108 -

नमस्ताम्राय चारुणाय च ॥

namastāmrāya cāruṇāya ca

We bow to he who is of copper red color and he who is the bright red of the love that brings the light of wisdom

- 109 -

नमः शङ्गवे च पशुपतये च ॥

namaḥ śaṇgave ca paśupataye ca

We bow to he who gives the blessing of auspiciousness and who is the lord of animals

- 110 -

नम उग्राय च भीमाय च ॥

nama ugrāya ca bhīmāya ca

We bow to he who is powerful and he who is tremendous

- 111 -

नमोऽग्रेवधाय च दूरेवधाय च ॥

namo grevadhāya ca dūrevadhāya ca

We bow to he who is foremost and who is boundless

- 112-

नमो हन्त्रे च हनीयसे च ॥

namo hantre ca hanīyase ca

We bow to he who is the destroyer of all and who holds weapons

- 113-

नमो वृक्षेभ्यो हरिकेशेभ्यः ॥

namo vṛkṣebhyo harikeśebyaḥ

We bow to he who is in the trees and who has divinely beautiful brown hair

- 114 -

नमस्ताराय ॥

namastārāya

We bow to he who shines in the stars

- 115 -

नमः शम्भवाय च मयोभवाय च ॥

namaḥ śambhavāya ca mayobhavāya ca

We bow to he whose being is in peace and who is the delight of all

- 116 -

नमः शङ्कराय च मयस्कराय च ॥

namaḥ śaṅkarāya ca mayaskarāya ca

We bow to he who is the cause of peace and who is the cause of all enjoyment

- 117 -

नमः शिवाय च शिवतराय च ॥

namaḥ śivāya ca śivatarāya ca

We bow to he who is the Consciousness of Infinite

Goodness and who is the most auspicious Consciousness of Infinite Goodness

- 118 -

नमः पार्याय चावार्याय च ॥

namaḥ pāryāya cāvāryāya ca

We bow to he who is the ultimate authority and beyond whom there is none else

- 119 -

नमः प्रतरणाय चोत्तरणाय च ॥

namaḥ prataraṇāya cottaraṇāya ca

We bow to he who elevates devotees and who is most superior

- 120 -

नमस्तीर्थ्याय च कूल्याय च ॥

namastīrṭhyāya ca kūlyāya ca

We bow to he who is the greatest place of pilgrimage and who is at the farthest extremity

- 121 -

नमः शष्प्याय च फेन्याय च ॥

namaḥ śaṣpyāya ca phenyāya ca

We bow to he who is in the grass and to he who is in the foam or froth

- 122 -

नमः सिकत्याय च प्रवाह्याय च ॥

namaḥ sikatyāya ca pravāhyāya ca

We bow to he who is in the sand and who is in the water's flow

- 123 -

नमः किंशिलाय च क्षयणाय च ॥

namaḥ kiṃśilāya ca kṣayaṇāya ca

We bow to he who is in the gravel and to he who lives quietly

- 124 -

नमः कपर्दिने च पुलस्तये च ॥

namaḥ kapardine ca pulastaye ca

We bow to he who has matted hair and he who preceeds the giver of law

- 125 -

नम इरिण्याय च प्रपथ्याय च ॥

nama iriṇyāya ca prapaṭhyāya ca

We bow to he who is in the desert and he who roams on the distant paths

- 126 -

नमो व्रज्याय च गोष्ठ्याय च ॥

namo vrajyāya ca goṣtyāya ca

We bow to he who illuminates lightning and he who is the refuge of men

- 127 -

नमस्तल्प्याय च गेह्याय च ॥

namastalpyāya ca gehyāya ca

We bow to he who is the resting place of all and who is the wealth of the house

- 128 -

नमो हृदय्याय च निवेष्प्याय च ॥

namo hṛdayyāya ca niveṣpyāya ca

We bow to he who lives in the hearts of all beings and who surrounds all existence

- 129 -

नमः काट्याय च गह्वरेष्ठाय च ॥

namaḥ kāṭyāya ca gahvareṣṭāya ca

We bow to he who is extremely deep and who is totally absorbed

- 130 -

नमः शुष्क्याय च हरित्याय च ॥

namaḥ śuṣkyāya ca harityāya ca

We bow to he who is withered or emaciated and who is pale (covered with ashes)

- 131 -

नमः पांसव्याय च रजस्याय च ॥

namaḥ pāṃsavyāya ca rajasyāya ca

We bow to he who is white like camphor and who fills the atmosphere

- 132 -

नमो लोप्याय चोलप्याय च ॥

namo lopyāya colapyāya ca

We bow to he who diminishes negativity and who is beyond negativity

- 133 -

नम ऊर्व्याय च सूर्व्याय च ॥

nama ūrvyāya ca sūrvyāya ca

We bow to he who is expansive and who is the beautiful container

- 134 -

नमः पर्णाय च पर्णशदाय च ॥

namaḥ parṇāya ca parṇaśadāya ca

We bow to he who is in green vegetation and who eats green vegetation

- 135 -

नम उद्गुरमाणाय चाभिघ्नते च ॥

nama udguramāṇāya cābhighate ca

We bow to he who raises his voice in excitement and who is always helpful

- 136 -

नम आखिदते च प्रखिदते च ॥

nama ākhidate ca prakhidate ca

We bow to he who draws all to himself and who sends all away from himself

- 137 -

नम इषुकृद्भ्यो धनुष्कृद्भ्यश्च वो नमः ॥

nama iṣukṛdbhyo dhanuṣkṛdbhyaśca vo namaḥ

We bow to he who arranges everything and who aims the bow at the target

- 138 -

नमो वः किरिकेभ्यो देवाना ँ॒ हृदयेभ्यः ॥

namo vaḥ kirikebhyo devānā guṃ hṛdayebhyaḥ

We bow to he who radiates divine light in the hearts of all

- 139 -

नमो विचिन्वत्केभ्यो देवाना ँ॒ हृदयेभ्यः ॥

namo vicinvatkebhyo devānā guṃ hṛdayebhyaḥ

We bow to he who illuminates divine discrimination in the hearts of all

- 140 -

नमो विक्षिणत्केभ्यो देवाना ँ॒ हृदयेभ्यः ॥

namo vikṣiṇatkebhyo devānā guṃ hṛdyebhyaḥ

We bow to he who replaces all evil with divinity in the hearts of all

- 141 -

नम आनिर्हतेभ्यः देवाना ँ॒ हृदयेभ्यः ॥

nama ānirhatebhyaḥ devānā guṃ hṛdayebhyaḥ

We bow to he who is the indestructible divine nature in the hearts of all

- 142 -

द्रापे अन्धसस्पते दरिद्र नीललोहित ।

आसां प्रजानमेषां पशूनां मा भेर्मारोङ्

मो च नः किंचनाममत् ॥

drāpe andhasaspate daridra nīlalohita
āsāṃ prajānameṣāṃ paśūnāṃ mā bhermāroṅḍ
mo ca naḥ kiṃcanāmamat

Oh Śiva with matted hair, who is blue and red, who presides over all living beings and animals, save all from the darkness of affliction, illness, and death.

- 143 -

इमा रुद्राय तवसे कपर्दिने क्षयाद्वीराय प्रभरामहे मतीः ।

यथा शमसद् द्विपदे चतुष्पदे

विश्वं पुष्टं ग्रामे अस्मिन्ननातुरम् ॥

imā rudrāya tavase kapardine kṣayād-
vīrāya prabharāmahe matīḥ
yathā śamsad dvipade catuṣpade
viśvaṃ puṣtaṃ grāme asminnanāturam

May the Reliever of Sufferings with matted hair, who destroys the pride of heroes, bestow upon us such resolution of thought as to nourish the entire universe with its villages of two footed and four footed beings.

- 144 -

या ते रुद्र शिवा तनूः शिवा विश्वाहा भेषजी ।

शिवा रुतस्य भेषजी तया नो मृड जीवसे ॥

yā te rudra śivā tanūḥ śivā viśvāhā bheṣajī
śivā rutasya bheṣajī tayā no mṛḍa jīvase

May that Rudra, Reliever of Sufferings, and Śivā, the Divine Mother as Infinite Consciousness, who embody the universe, heal us from all maladies and bestow upon us a delightful life.

\- 145 -

परि नो रुद्रस्य हेतिर्वृणाक्तु परि त्वेषस्य दुर्मतिरघायोः ।
अवस्थिरा मघवद्भ्यस्तनुष्व मीढ्वस्तोकाय तनयाय मृड ॥

pari no rudrasya hetir
vṛṇāktu pari tveṣasya durmatiraghāyoḥ
avasthirā maghavadbhyastanuṣva
mīḍhvastokāya tanayāya mṛḍa

Oh Rudra, Reliever of Sufferings, remove from us all enmity. Oh Destroyer of Selfishness, eradicate all violence. Bring us to your stillness so that we may all share in your delight.

\- 146 -

मीढुष्टम शिवतम शिवो नः सुमना भव ।
परमे वृक्ष आयुधं निधाय कृत्तिं
वसान आचर पिनाकं बिभ्रदा गहि ॥

mīḍhuṣtama śivatama śivo naḥ sumanā bhava
parame vṛkṣa āyudhaṃ nidhāya kṛttiṃ
vasāna ācara pinākaṃ bibhradā gahi

Oh most bountiful Śiva, give us minds filled with excellence. Come bearing your trident and make war upon the residence of the cruel and pitiless.

\- 147 -

विकिरिद्र विलोहित नमस्ते अस्तु भगवः ।
यास्ते सहस्रं हेतयोऽन्यमस्मन्नि वपन्तु ताः ॥

vikiridra vilohita namaste astu bhagavaḥ
yāste sahasraṃ hetayo-nyamasmanni vapantu tāḥ

We bow to you who is free from passion, the Supreme Lord, whose intrinsic nature is purity. With the thousands of weapons at your command protect us from all enmity.

- 148 -

सहस्राणि सहस्रशो बाह्वोस्तव हेतयः ।

तामाभीशानो भगवः पराचीना मुखा कृधि ॥

sahasrāṇi sahasraśo bāhvostava hetayaḥ
tāmābhīśāno bhagavaḥ parācīnā mukhā kṛdhi

Oh Supreme Lord, with thousands of weapons at your command, protect us from all enmity with your every capacity.

- 149 -

असंख्याता सहस्राणि ये रुद्रा अधि भूम्याम् ।

तेषाꣳ सहस्रयोजनेऽव धन्वानि तन्मसि ॥

asaṃkhyātā sahasrāṇi ye rudrā adhi bhūmyām
teṣā guṃ sahasrayojane-va dhanvāni tanmasi

Reliever of Sufferings, infinite in nature, with thousands of manifestations over and above the earth. Thus we roam in distant places extending for thousands of miles and use the weapons of knowledge for the removal of ignorance.

- 150 -

अस्मिन् महत्यर्णवेऽन्तरिक्षे भवा अधि ।

तेषाꣳ सहस्रयोजनेऽव धन्वानि तन्मसि ॥

asmin mahatyarṇave-ntarikṣe bhavā adhi
teṣā guṃ sahasrayojane-va dhanvāni tanmasi

You are over and above the great sea, the atmosphere, and all that has come into existence. Thus we roam in distant places extending for thousands of miles and use the weapons of knowledge for the removal of ignorance.

- 151 -

नीलग्रीवाः शितिकण्ठाः दिवं रुद्रा उपश्रिताः ।

तेषाꣳ सहस्रयोजनेऽव धन्वानि तन्मसि ॥

nīlagrīvāḥ śitikaṇṭhāḥ divaṃ rudrā upaśritāḥ
teṣā guṃ sahasrayojane-va dhanvāni tanmasi

Oh Reliever of Sufferings, with a dark blue neck, you are the support of the heavens. Thus we roam in distant places extending for thousands of miles and use the weapons of knowledge for the removal of ignorance.

- 152 -

नीलग्रीवाः शितिकण्ठाः शर्वा अधः क्षमाचराः ।

तेषा ँ सहस्रयोजनेऽव धन्वानि तन्मसि ॥

nīlagrīvāḥ śitikaṇṭhāḥ śarvā adhaḥ kṣamācarāḥ
teṣā gum sahasrayojane-va dhanvāni tanmasi

Oh one with a dark blue neck, you slay with arrows the fears of the lower regions beneath the earth. Thus we roam in distant places extending for thousands of miles and use the weapons of knowledge for the removal of ignorance.

- 153 -

ये वृक्षेषु शष्पिञ्जरा नीलग्रीवा विलोहिताः ।

तेषा ँ सहस्रयोजनेऽव धन्वानि तन्मसि ॥

ye vṛkṣeṣu śaṣpiñjarā nīlagrīvā vilohītāḥ
teṣā gum sahasrayojane-va dhanvāni tanmasi

Oh you who are without passion, with a blue neck, you are in the trees, both young and old. Thus we roam in distant places extending for thousands of miles and use the weapons of knowledge for the removal of ignorance.

- 154 -

ये भूतानामधिपतयो विशिखासः कपर्दिनः ।

तेषा ँ सहस्रयोजनेऽव धन्वानि तन्मसि ॥

ye bhūtānāmadhipatayo viśikhāsaḥ kapardinaḥ
teṣā gum sahasrayojane-va dhanvāni tanmasi

Those with matted hair and those with no hair at all, regard you as the Supreme Lord of all beings. Thus we roam in distant places extending for thousands of miles and use the weapons of knowledge for the removal of ignorance.

\- 155 -

ये पथां पथिरक्षय ऐलबृदा आयुर्युधः ।

तेषाꣳ सहस्रयोजनेऽव धन्वानि तन्मसि ॥

ye pathāṃ pathirakṣaya ailabṛdā āyuryudhaḥ
teṣā guṃ sahasrayojane-va dhanvāni tanmasi

All travellers on the path take refuge from the battles of life in you. Thus we roam in distant places extending for thousands of miles and use the weapons of knowledge for the removal of ignorance.

\- 156 -

ये तीर्थानि प्रचरन्ति सृकाकस्ता निषङ्गिणः ।

तेषाꣳ सहस्रयोजनेऽव धन्वानि तन्मसि ॥

ye tīrthāni pracaranti sṛkākastā niṣaṅgiṇaḥ
teṣā guṃ sahasrayojane-va dhanvāni tanmasi

Oh you without attachment, those who visit the pilgrimage places and speak of you hold the arrows of concentration in their hands. Thus we roam in distant places extending for thousands of miles and use the weapons of knowledge for the removal of ignorance.

\- 157 -

येऽन्नेषु विविध्यन्ति पात्रेषु पिबतो जनान् ।

तेषाꣳ सहस्रयोजनेऽव धन्वानि तन्मसि ॥

ye-nneṣu vividhyanti pātreṣu pibato janān
teṣā guṃ sahasrayojane-va dhanvāni tanmasi

You are in the food which has been prepared and in the drink which people drink. Thus we roam in distant places extending for thousands of miles and use the weapons of knowledge for the removal of ignorance.

\- 158 -

यऽएतावन्तश्च भूयांसश्च दिशो रुद्रा वितस्थिरे ।

तेषाꣳ सहस्रयोजनेऽव धन्वानि तन्मसि ॥

y-etāvantaśca bhūyāṃ saśca diśo rudrā vitasthire
teṣā guṃ sahasrayojane-va dhanvāni tanmasi
Oh Rudra, the truth of your being is so great that you have spread out in all directions becoming everything. Thus we roam in distant places extending for thousands of miles and use the weapons of knowledge for the removal of ignorance.

- 159 -

नमोऽस्तु रुद्रेभ्यो ये दिवि येषां वर्षमिषवः ।

तेभ्यो दश प्राचीर्दश दक्षिणा

दश प्रतीचीर्दशोदीचीर्दशोर्ध्वाः ।

तेभ्यो नमो अस्तु ते नोऽवन्तु ते नो मृडयन्तु

ते यं द्विष्मो यश्च नो द्वेष्टि तमेषां जम्भे दध्मः ॥

namo-stu rudrebhyo ye divi yeṣāṃ varṣamiṣavaḥ
tebhyo daśa prācīr daśa dakṣiṇā
daśa pratīcīr daśodīcīr daśordhvāḥ
tebhyo namo astu te no-vantu te no mṛḍayantu
te yaṃ dviṣmo yaśce no dveṣti tameṣāṃ
jambhe dadhmaḥ
We bow to the forms of Rudra in the heavens who cause the rains to fall. To them, ten to the east, ten to the south, ten to the west, ten to the north, ten above. May these forms of Rudra protect us and fill us with delight. We send all conflict to Rudra for it to be destroyed.

- 160 -

नमोऽस्तु रुद्रेभ्यो येऽन्तरिक्षे येषां वात इषवः ।

तेभ्यो दश प्राचीर्दश दक्षिणा

दश प्रतीचीर्दशोदीचीर्दशोर्ध्वाः ।

तेभ्यो नमो अस्तु ते नोऽवन्तु ते नो मृडयन्तु

ते यं द्विष्मो यश्च नो द्वेष्टि तमेषां जम्भे दध्मः ॥

namo-stu rudrebhyo ye-ntarikṣe yeṣāṃ vāta iṣavaḥ
tebhyo daśa prācir daśa dakṣiṇā daśa pratīcīr
daśodīcīr daśordhvāḥ
tebhyo namo astu te no-vantu te no mṛḍayantu
te yaṃ dviṣmo yaśce no dveṣti tameṣāṃ
jambhe dadhmaḥ

We bow to the forms of Rudra in the atmosphere who cause the winds to blow. To them, ten to the east, ten to the south, ten to the west, ten to the north, ten above. May these forms of Rudra, protect us and fill us with delight. We send all conflict to Rudra for it to be destroyed.

\- 161 -

नमोऽस्तु रुद्रेभ्यो ये पृथिव्यां येषमन्न मिषवः ।
तेभ्यो दश प्राचीर्दश दक्षिणा
दश प्रतीचीर्दशोदीचीर्दशोर्ध्वाः ।
तेभ्यो नमो अस्तु ते नोऽवन्तु ते नो मृडयन्तु
ते यं द्विष्मो यश्च नो द्वेष्टि तमेषां जम्भे दध्मः ॥

namo-stu rudrebhyo ye pṛthivyāṃ yeṣamanna
miṣavaḥ
tebhyo daśa prācīr daśa dakṣiṇā daśa pratīcīr
daśodīcīr daśordhvāḥ
tebhyo namo astu te no-vantu te no mṛḍayantu
te yaṃ dviṣmo yaśce no dveṣti tameṣāṃ
jambhe dadhmaḥ

We bow to the forms of Rudra on the earth who take delight and nourishment in food. To them, ten to the east, ten to the south, ten to the west, ten to the north, ten above. May these forms of Rudra, protect us and fill us with delight. We send all conflict to Rudra for it to be destroyed.

इति पञ्चमोऽध्यायः

iti pañcāmo-dhyāyaḥ

Thus ends the fifth chapter.

* Ten means our ten finger tips placed together in bowing (our utmost respect), or it means the space of ten fingers breadth (the entire heart area or the fullness of my heart), or it means our ten indriyas or senses offered to the God in every direction (five organs of action and five organs or knowledge).

Chapter 6

हरिः ॐ

hariḥ oṃ

Praise to oṃ

\- 1 -

वयं सोम व्रते तव मनस्तनूषु बिभ्रतः ।

प्रजावन्तः सचेमहि ॥

vayaṃ soma vrate tava manastanūṣu bibhrataḥ prajāvantaḥ sacemahi

Oh Lord of Devotion who shines like the Moon, you have bestowed upon us these bodies as the vehicle to carry the mind, that we may delight in the vow to serve all beings born.

\- 2 -

एष ते रुद्र भागः सह स्वस्राम्बिकया तं जुषस्व स्वाहैष ते

रुद्र भाग आखुस्ते पशुः ॥

eṣa te rudra bhāgaḥ saha svasrāmbikayā taṃ juṣasva svāhaiṣa te rudra bhāga ākhuste paśuḥ

Oh Destroyer of all sin, Rudra, Reliever of Sufferings, you who have the wealth of pure being, come as the Father of Pure Being, come as the Father of the Universe and purify us. I am One with God! Oh, Rudra, establish your pure truth within us and destroy our animalistic nature.

\- 3 -

अव रुद्रमदीमह्यव देवं त्र्यम्बकम् ।

यथा नो वस्यसस्करद्यथा नः श्रेयसस्करद्यथा नो

व्यवसाययात् ॥

ava rudramadīmahyava devaṃ tryambakam yathā no vasyasaskaradyathā naḥ śreyasaskaradyathā no vyavasāyayāt

We are worshipping Rudra, the Reliever of Sufferings, as the Father of the Three Worlds, and pray that he bless us with peace, unselfish love, and perfection in our every endeavor.

- 4 -

भेषजमसि भेषजं गवेऽश्वाय पुरुषाय भेषजम् ।

सुखं मेषाय मेष्यै ॥

bheṣajamasi bheṣajaṃ gave-śvāya
puruṣāya bheṣajam
sukhaṃ meṣāya meṣyai

You are the cure of all cures, for cows, horses, ewes, and humans. You are the medicine. Give peace and comfort.

- 5 -

त्र्यम्बकं यजामहे सुगन्धिं पतिवेदनम् ।

उर्व्वारुकमिव बन्धनादितोमुक्षीयमामुतः ।

tryambakaṃ yajāmahe sugandhiṃ pativedanam
urvvārukamiva bandhanāditomukṣīyamāmutaḥ

We adore the Father of the three worlds, of excellent fame, Grantor of Increase. As a cucumber is released from its bondage to the stem, so may we be freed from Death to dwell in immortality.

- 6 -

त्र्यम्बकं यजामहे सुगन्धिं पुष्टिवर्द्धनम् ।

उर्व्वारुकमिव बन्धनान्मृत्योर्म्मुक्षीयमामृतात् ॥

tryambakaṃ yajāmahe
sugandhiṃ puṣṭivarddhanam
urvvārukamiva bandhanānmṛtyormmukṣīyamāmṛtāt

We adore the Father of the three worlds, of excellent fame, Grantor of Increase. As a cucumber is released from its bondage to the stem, so may we be freed from Death to dwell in immortality.

- 7 -

एतत्ते रुद्रावसं तेन परो मूजवतोऽतीहि ।

अवततधन्वा पिनाकावसः कृत्तिवासा

अहिंसन्नः शिवोऽतीहि ॥

etatte rudrāvasaṃ tena paro mūjavato-tīhi
avatatadhanvā pinākāvasaḥ kṛttivāsā
ahiṃ sannaḥ śivo-tīhi

Hey Rudra, Reliever of Sufferings, come with your bow and your trident and protect us from all sin. Destroy all enmity and establish us in truth.

- 8 -

त्र्यायुषं जमदग्नेः कश्यपस्य त्र्यायुषम् ।

यद्देवेषु त्र्यायुषं तन्नोऽअस्तु त्र्यायुषम् ॥

tryāyuṣaṃ jamadagneḥ kaśayapasya tryāyuṣam
yaḍeveṣu tryāyuṣaṃ tanno-astu tryāyuṣam

Three lifetimes filled with bliss is the blessing from Jamadagne, from Kaśyapa three lifetimes more. All the Gods and Goddesses grant three lifetimes filled with bliss. Let that be unto you, three lifetimes filled with bliss.

- 9 -

शिवो नामासि स्वधितिस्ते पिता

नमस्ते अस्तु मा मा हिंसीः ।

नि वर्त्तयाम्यायुषेऽन्नाद्याय प्रजननाय

रायस्पोषाय सुप्रजास्त्वाय सुवीर्याय ॥

śivo nāmāsi svadhitiste pitā
namaste astu mā mā hiṃsīḥ
ni varttayāmyāyuṣe-nnādyāya prajananāya
rāyaspoṣāya suprajāstvāya suvīryaya

We are bowing to you who is established as the Father of the Universe, Śiva. We are bowing to you who destroys all enmity and violence. We bow to you who are eternal life, the form of the attitude of truth, the welfare of the perceivable universe, the form of increase in the universe, the supreme meaning of wealth and the discipline by which it is attained. We bow to you the grantor of the greatest welfare for all, who gives the capacity for all to act in truth, who empowers all with the intrinsic nature of peace, and the attitude of godliness, we bow to you.

इति षष्ठोऽध्यायः

iti ṣaṣṭho-dhyāyaḥ

Thus ends the sixth chapter.

Chapter 7

हरिः ॐ

hariḥ oṃ

Praise to oṃ

- 1 -

उग्रश्च भीमश्च ध्वान्तश्च धुनिश्च ।

सासह्वाँश्चाभियुग्वा च विक्षिपः स्वाहा ॥

ugraśca bhīmaśca ḍhvāntaśca dhuniśca
sāsahvāṁścābhiyugvā ca vikṣipaḥ svāhā

We worship He who is terrible, who is formidable, who is darkness (unknowable), the consecrated fire, whose greatness has spread through all existence, I am One with God.

- 2 -

अग्निं हृदयेनाशनिं हृदयाग्रेण

पशुपतिं कृत्स्नहृदयेन भवं यक्ना ।

शर्वं मतस्नाभ्यामीशानं मन्युना

महादेवमन्तःपर्शव्येनोग्रं देवं

वनिष्ठुना वसिष्ठहनुः शिङ्गीनि कोश्याभ्याम् ॥

agniṃ hṛdayenāśaniṃ hṛdayāgreṇa
paśupatiṃ kṛtsnahṛdayena bhavaṃ yaknā
śarvaṃ matasnābhyāmīśānaṃ manyunā
mahādevamanataḥparśavyenograṃ devaṃ
vaniṣtunā vasiṣtahanuḥ śiṅgīni kośyābhyām

With our pure devotion we call Agni, the light of purification, to our hearts. We call the God with the thunderbolt to our hearts. With a full heart we call the Lord of Animals, who is all existence, who is pure being in the hearts of all, the Supreme Lord who rules over all, the great lord who is the perceivable universe, who is the offering in sacrifice, who is the most excellent and most wealthy, who is perceived as the storehouse of treasure.

- 3 -

उग्रंल्लोहितेन मित्रं सौव्रत्येन रुद्रं दौर्व्रत्येनेन्द्रं

प्रक्रीडेन मरुतो बलेन साध्यान् प्रमुदा ।

भवस्य कण्ठ्यं रुद्रस्यान्तः

पाश्र्व्यं महादेवस्य

यकृच्छर्वस्य वनिष्ठुः पशुपतेः पुरीतत् ॥

ugramlohitena mitraṃ sauvratyena rudraṃ daurvratyenendraṃ
prakrīḍena maruto balena sāḍhyān pramudā
bhavasya kaṇṭhyaṃ rudrasyāntaḥ
pāśarvyaṃ mahādevasya
yakṛccharvasya vaniṣṭuḥ paśupateḥ purītat

With the red of pure love we worship the Formidable One. With purity we worship Friendship. With great detachment we worship the Reliever of Sufferings. With most excellent actions we worship Indra, the Rule of the Pure. With great strength we worship the Maruts, the Winds of Freedom. With the greatest devotion we worship the God of efficiency. We worship the Spirit of All Being in the throat, the Reliever of Sufferings on the two sides, the Great God in the liver or midsection, and the most generous Lord of Animals in the heart.

- 4 -

लोमभ्यः स्वाहा लोमभ्यः स्वाहा त्वचे स्वाहा त्वचे स्वाहा

लोहिताय स्वाहा लोहिताय स्वहा मेदोभ्यः स्वाहा मेदोभ्यः स्वाहा ।

मांसेभ्यः स्वाहा मांसेभ्यः स्वाहा स्नावभ्यः स्वाहा स्नावभ्यः
स्वाहाऽस्थभ्यः स्वाहाऽस्थभ्यः स्वाहा मज्ज्भ्यः स्वाहा
मज्ज्भ्यः स्वाहा रेतसे स्वाहा पायवे स्वाहा ॥

lomabhyaḥ svāhā lomabhyaḥ svāhā tvace svāhā tvace svāhā lohitāya svāhā lohitāya svahā medobhyaḥ svāhā medobhyaḥ svāhā māṃsebhyaḥ svāhā māṃsebhyaḥ svāhā snāvabhyaḥ svāhā snāvabhyaḥ svāhā-sthabhyaḥ svāhā-sthabhyaḥ svāhā majjabhyaḥ svāhā majjabhyaḥ svāhā retase svāhā pāyave svāhā

to the hair
to the skin
to the blood
to the fat
to the meat
to the nerves
to the tendons
to the bones
to the seeds of life
to the anus

- 5 -

आयासाय स्वाहा प्रायासाय स्वाहा संयासाय स्वाहा
वियासाय स्वाहोद्यासाय स्वाहा ।
शुचेस्वाहा शोचते स्वाहा शोचमानाय स्वाहा
शोकाय स्वाहा ॥

āyāsāya svāhā prāyāsāya svāhā saṃyāsāya svāhā viyasāya svāhodyāsāya svāhā śuce svāhā śocate svāhā śocamānāya svāhā śokāya svāhā

to exertion
to atonement
to effort
to exclude the unnecessary
to raise one's self up
to purity
to greater purity
to purity of mind
to purity of body

- 6 -

तपसे स्वाहा तप्यते स्वाहा तप्यमानाय स्वाहा तप्ताय स्वाहा घर्माय स्वाहा ।
निष्कृत्यै स्वाहा प्रायश्चित्यै स्वाहा भेषजाय स्वाहा ॥

tapase svāhā tapyate svāhā tapyamānāya svāhā taptāya svāhā gharmāya svāhā
niṣkṛtyai svāhā prāyaścityai svāhā bheṣajāya svāhā

to purifying austerities
to the performer of purifying austerities
to the mind of purifying austerities
to the light of the sacrificial fire
to expiation of all faults
to acts of purification
to the healing

- 7 -

यमाय स्वाहाऽन्तकाय स्वाहा मृत्यवे स्वाहा ।
ब्रह्मणे स्वाहा ब्रह्महत्यायै स्वाहा विश्वेभ्यो देवेभ्यः स्वाहा द्यावापृथिवीभ्यां स्वाहा ॥

yamāya svāhā-ntakāya sāhā mṛtyave svāhā
brahmaṇe svāhā brahmahatyāyai svāhā viśvebhyo devebhyaḥ svāyā dyāvāpṛthivībhyāṃ svāhā

to control
to the ultimate
to death
to the greatest divinity
to the lowest divinity
to all the Gods of the universe
to heaven and earth

इति सप्तमोऽध्यायः

iti saptamo-dhyāyaḥ
Thus ends the seventh chapter.

Chapter 8

हरिः ॐ

hariḥ oṃ

Praise to oṃ

\- 1 -

वाजश्च मे प्रसवश्च मे प्रयतिश्च मे प्रसितिश्च मे ॥ धीतिश्च मे क्रतुश्च मे स्वरश्च मे श्लोकश्च मे ॥ श्रवश्च मे श्रुतिश्च मे ज्योतिश्च मे स्वश्च मे ॥ यज्ञेन कल्पन्ताम् ॥

vājaśca me prasavaśca me prayatiśca me prasitiśca me || dhītiśca me kratuśca me svaraśca me ślokaśca me || śravaśca me śrutiśca me jyotiśca me svaśca me || yajñena kalpantāṃ ||

Strength is within me, and increase is within me, and inclination is within me, and thought is within me, and mental power is within me, and heaven is within me, and verses of praise are within me, and renown is within me, and sacred knowledge is within me, and light is within me, and my own self is within me, by means of sacrifice I conceive that all is within me.

\- 2 -

प्राणश्च मेऽपानश्च मे व्यानश्च मेऽसुश्च मे ॥ चित्तं च म आधीतं च मे वाक् च मे मनश्च मे ॥ चक्षुश्च मे श्रोत्रं च मे दक्षश्च मे बलं च मे ॥ यज्ञेन कल्पन्ताम् ॥

prāṇaśca me-pānaśca me vyānaśca me-suśca me || cittaṃ ca ma ādhītaṃ ca me vāk ca me manaśca me || cakṣuśca me śrotraṃ ca me dakṣaśca me balaṃ ca me || yajñena kalpantāṃ ||

The inflowing breath is within me, and the outflowing breath is within me, and the retained breath is within me, and the breath of life is within me, and consciousness is within me, and contemplation is within me, and vibrations are within me, and mind is within me, and sight is within me, and sound is within me, and ability is within me, and force is within me, by means of sacrifice I conceive that all is within me.

\- 3 -

ओजश्च मे सहश्च म आत्मा च मे तनूश्च मे ॥ शर्म च मे वर्म च मेऽङ्गानि च मेऽस्थीनि च मे ॥ परूंषि च मे शरीराणि च म आयुश्च मे जरा च मे ॥ यज्ञेन कल्पन्ताम् ॥

ojaśca me sahaśca ma ātmā ca me tanūśca me || śarma ca me varma ca me-ṅgāni ca me-sthīni ca me || parūṃ ṣi ca me śarīrāṇi ca ma āyuśca me jarā ca me || yajñena kalpantāṃ ||

Energy is within me, and power is within me, and the Self is within me, and the body is within me, and delight is within me, and protection is within me, and limbs are within me, and bones are within me, and this physical form is within me, and humanity is within me, and maturity is within me, by means of sacrifice I conceive that all is within me.

\- 4 -

ज्यैष्ठ्यं च म आधिपत्यं च मे मन्युश्च मे भाश्च मे ॥ मश्च में भश्च मे जेमा च मे महिमा च मे ॥ वरिमा च मे प्रथिमा च मे वर्षिमा च मे द्राघिमा च मे ॥ वृद्धं च मे वृद्धिश्च मे ॥ यज्ञेन कल्पन्ताम् ॥

jyaiṣṭyaṃ ca ma ādhipatyaṃ ca me manyuśca me bhāśca me || maśca me jemā ca me mahimā ca me || varimā ca me prathimā ca me varṣimā ca me drāghimā ca me || vṛddhiṃ ca me vṛiddhiśca me || yajñena kalpantāṃ ||

Preeminence is within me, and leadership is within me, and zealousness is within me, and brightness is within me, and splendor is within me, and food is within me, and greatness is within me, and excellence is within me, and magnitude is within me, and breadth is within me, and length is within me, and increase is within me, and development is within me, by means of sacrifice I conceive that all is within me.

- 5 -

सत्यं च मे श्रद्धा च मे जगच्च मे ॥ धनं च मे विश्वं च मे महश्च मे ॥ क्रीडा च मे मोदश्च मे जातं च जनिष्यमाणं च मे ॥ सूक्तं च मे सुकृतं च मे ॥ यज्ञेन कल्पन्ताम् ॥

satyaṃ ca me śraddhā ca me jagacca me || dhanaṃ ca me viśvaṃ ca me mahaśca me || krīḍā ca me modaśca me jātaṃ ca janiṣyamāṇaṃ ca me || sūktaṃ ca me sukṛtaṃ ca me || yajñena kalpantāṃ ||

Truth is within me, and faith is within me, and the world is within me, and wealth is within me, and the universe is within me, and sacrifice is within me, and play is within me, and joy is within me, and all beings born are within me, and all creatures born are within me, and hymns are within me, and excellent acts are within me, by means of sacrifice I conceive that all is within me.

- 6 -

ऋतं च मेऽमृतं च मेऽयक्ष्मं च मे ॥ नामयच्च मे जीवातुश्च मे दीर्घायुत्वं च मे ॥ नमित्रं च मेऽभयं च मे सुखं च मे ॥ शयणं च मे सूषाश्च मे सूदिनं च मे ॥ यज्ञेन कल्पन्ताम् ॥

ṛtaṃ ca me-mṛtaṃ ca me-yakṣmaṃ ca me || nāmayacca me jīvātuśca me dīrghayutvaṃ ca me || namitraṃ ca me-bhayaṃ ca me sukhaṃ ca me || śayaṇaṃ ca me sūṣāśca me sūdinaṃ ca me || yajñena kalpantāṃ ||

The imperishable is within me, and the nectar of Bliss is within me, and good health is within me, and welfare is within me, and a satisfactory life is within me, and longevity is within me, and only friendly beings are within me, and freedom from fear is within me, and happiness is within me, and rest is within me, and excellent subsistence is within me, and excellent days are within me, by means of sacrifice I conceive that all is within me.

- 7 -

यन्ता च मे धर्ता च मे क्षेमश्च मे ॥ धृतिश्च मे विश्वं च मे महश्च मे ॥ संविच्च मे ज्ञात्रं च मे सूश्च मे ॥ प्रसूश्च मे सीरं च मे लयश्च मे ॥ यज्ञेन कल्पन्ताम् ॥

yantā ca me dharta ca me kṣemaśca me ॥ dhṛtiśca me viśvaṃ ca me mahaśca me ॥ saṃvicca me jñātraṃ ca me sūśca me ॥ prasūśca me sīraṃ ca me layaśca me ॥ yajñena kalpantāṃ ॥

Direction is within me, and creative capacity is within me, and happiness is within me, and constancy is within me, and the universe is within me, and sacrifice is within me, and knowledge is within me, and wisdom is within me, and productivity is within me, and yielding is within me, and absorption of the mind in the deepest concentration is within me, by means of sacrifice I conceive that all is within me.

- 8 -

शं च मे मयश्च मे प्रियं च मे ॥ नुकामश्च मे कामश्च मे सौमनसश्च मे ॥ भगश्च मे द्रविणं च मे भद्रं च मे ॥ श्रेयश्च मे वसीयश्च मे यशश्च मे ॥ यज्ञेन कल्पन्ताम् ॥

śaṃ ca me mayaśca me priyaṃ ca me ॥ nukāmaśca me kāmaśca me saumanaśca me ॥ bhagaśca me draviṇaṃ ca me bhadraṃ ca me ॥ śreyaśca me vasīyaśca me yaśaśca me ॥ yajñena kalpantāṃ ॥

Bliss is within me, and delight is within me, and love is within me, and all that is desired is within me, and satisfaction is within me, and complete prosperity is within me, and substance is within me, and excellence is within me, and even better is within me, and even greater bliss is within me, and glory is within me, by means of sacrifice I conceive that all is within me.

- 9 -

ऊर्क् च मे सूनृता च मे पयश्च मे ॥ रसश्च मे घृतं च मे मधु च मे ॥ सग्धिश्च मे सपीतिश्च मे कृषिश्च मे ॥ वृष्टिश्च मे जैत्रं च म औद्भिद्यं च मे ॥ यज्ञेन कल्पन्ताम् ॥

ūrk ca me sūnṛtā ca me payaśca me ǁ rasaśca me ghṛtaṃ ca me madhu ca me ǁ sagidhiśca me spītiśca me kṛṣiśca me ǁ vṛṣṭiśca me jaitraṃ ca ma audbhidyaṃ ca me ǁ yajñena kalpantāṃ ǁ

Vigor is within me, and sincerity is within me, and vital spirit is within me, and appreciation is within me, and clarity is within me, and sweetness is within me, and sharing food is within me, and sharing drink is within me, and cultivation is within me, and the rain is within me, and success is within me, and victory is within me, by means of sacrifice I conceive that all is within me.

- 10 -

रयिश्च मे रायश्च मे पुष्टं च मे ॥ पुष्टिश्च मे विभु च मे प्रभु च मे ॥ पूर्णं च मे पूर्णतरं च मे कुयवं च मे ॥ क्षितं च मेऽन्नं च मेऽक्षुच्च मे ॥ यज्ञेन कल्पन्ताम् ॥

rayiśca me rāyaśca me puṣṭaṃ ca me ǁ puṣṭiśca me vibhu ca me prabhu ca me ǁ pūrṇaṃ ca me pūrṇataraṃ ca me kuyavaṃ ca me ǁ kṣitaṃ ca me-nnaṃ ca me-kṣucca me ǁ yajñena kalpantāṃ ǁ

Wealth is within me, and kings are within me, and nourishment is within me, and enrichment is within me, and manifestation is within me, and ability is within me, and fullness is within me, and completeness is within me, and the transitory is within me, and food is within me, and satiation is within me, by means of sacrifice I conceive that all is within me.

- 11 -

वित्तं च मे वेद्यं च मे भूतं च मे ॥ भविष्यच्च मे सुगं च मे सुपथ्यं च म ॥ ऋद्धं च म ऋद्धिश्च मे क्लृप्तं च मे ॥ क्लृप्तिश्च मे मतिश्च मे सुमतिश्च मे ॥ यज्ञेन कल्पन्ताम् ॥

vittaṃ ca me vedyaṃ ca me bhūtaṃ ca me ll bhaviṣyacca me sugaṃ ca me supathyaṃ ca ma ll ṛddhaṃ ca ma ṛddhiśca me klṛptaṃ ca me ll klṛptiśca me matiśca me sumatiśca me ll yajñena kapantām ll

Gain is within me, and what is to be known is within me, and being is within me, and becoming is within me, and elegance is within me, and the good path is within me, and growth is within me, and grandeur is within me, and achievement is within me, and contrivance is within me, and understanding is within me, and good judgement is within me, by means of sacrifice I conceive that all is within me.

- 12 -

व्रीहयश्च मे यवाश्च मे माषाश्च मे ॥ तिलाश्च मे मुद्गाश्च मे खल्वाश्च मे ॥ प्रियङ्गवश्च मेऽणवश्च मे श्यामाकाश्च मे ॥ नीवाराश्च मे गोधूमाश्च मे मसूराश्च मे ॥ यज्ञेन कल्पन्ताम् ॥

brīhayaśca me yavāśca me māṣāśca me ll tilāśca me mudgāśca me khalvāśca me ll priyaṅgavaśca me-ṇvaśca me śyāmākāśca me ll nīvārāśca me godhūmāśca me masūrāśca me ll yajñena kalpantāṃ ll

Rice is within me, and barley is within me, and vegetables are within me, and sesame is within me, and beans are within me, and grains are within me, and millet is within me, and Panicum Milliaceum is within me, and Panicum Frumentaceum is within me, and wild rice is within me, and wheat is within me, and lentils are within me, by means of sacrifice I conceive that all is within me.

- 13 -

अश्मा च मे मृत्तिका च मे गिरश्च मे ॥ पर्वताश्च मे सिकताश्च मे वनस्पतयश्च मे ॥ हिरण्यं च मे यश्च मे श्यामं च मे ॥ लोहं च मे सीसं च मे त्रपु च मे ॥ यज्ञेन कल्पन्ताम् ॥

aśmā ca me mṛttikā ca me giraśca me || parvatāśca me sikatāśca me vanaspatayaśca me || hiraṇyaṃ ca me-yaśca me śyāmaṃ ca me || lohaṃ ca me sīsaṃ ca me trapu ca me || yajñena kalpantāṃ ||

Stone is within me, and clay is within me, and hills are within me, and mountains are within me, and pebbles are within me, and trees are within me, and gold is within me, and bronze is within me, and copper is within me, and iron is within me, and lead is within me, and tin is within me, by means of sacrifice I conceive that all is within me.

- 14 -

अग्निश्च म आपश्च मे वीरुधश्च म ॥ ओषधयश्च मे कृष्टपच्याश्च मे ऽकृष्टपच्याश्च मे ॥ ग्राम्याश्च मे पशव आरण्याश्च मे वित्तं च मे ॥ वित्तिश्च मे भूतं च मे भूतिश्च मे ॥ यज्ञेन कल्पन्ताम् ॥

agniśca ma āpaśca me vīrudhaśca ma || oṣdhayaśca me kṛṣṭapacyāśca me-kṛṣṭapacyāśca me || grāmyāśca me paśava āraṇyāśca me vittaṃ ca me || vittiśca me bhūtaṃ ca me bhūtiśca me || yajñena kalpantāṃ ||

Fire is within me, and water is within me, and creepers are within me, and plants are within me, and plants with cultivated fruit are within me, and plants with wild fruits are within me, and domestic animals are within me, and wild animals are within me, and substance is within me, and future substance is within me, and possessions are within me, and benevolence is within me, by means of sacrifice I conceive that all is within me.

- 15 -

वसु च मे वसतिश्च मे कर्म च मे ॥ शक्तिश्च मेऽर्थश्च म एमश्च म ॥ इत्या च मे गतिश्च मे ॥ यज्ञेन कल्पन्ताम् ॥

vasu ca me vasatiśca me karma ca me ǁ śaktiśca mer-thaśca ma emaśca ma ǁ ityā ca me gatiśca me ǁ yajñena kalpantām ǁ

The treasure is within me, and the abode is within me, and action is within me, and energy is within me, and all name-able objects are within me, and the path is within me, and from this moment on is within me, and motion is within me, by means of sacrifice I conceive that all is within me.

- 16 -

अग्निश्च म इन्द्रश्च मे ॥ सोमश्च म इन्द्रश्च मे ॥ सविता च म इन्द्रश्च मे ॥ सरस्वती च म इन्द्रश्च मे ॥ पूषा च म इन्द्रश्च मे ॥ बृहस्पतिश्च म इन्द्रश्च मे ॥ यज्ञेन कल्पन्ताम् ॥

agniśca ma indraśca me ǁ somaśca me indraścha me ǁ savitā ca ma indraśca me ǁ sarasvatī ca ma indraśca me ǁ pūṣā ca ma indraśca me ǁ bṛhaspatiśca ma indraśca me ǁ yajñena kalpantāṃ ǁ

And the Light of Meditation is within me, and the Rule of the Pure is within me, and Unqualified Devotion is within me, and the Rule of the Pure is within me, and the Light of Wisdom is within me, and the Rule of the Pure is within me, and the Spirit of All- Pervading Knowledge is within me, and the Rule of the Pure is within me, and The Search for Truth is within me, and the Rule of the Pure is within me, and the Spirit of all Bliss is within me, and Rule of the Pure is within me, by means of sacrifice I conceive that all is within me.

- 17 -

मित्रश्च म इन्द्रश्च मे ॥ वरुणश्च म इन्द्रश्च मे ॥ धाता च म इन्द्रश्च मे ॥ त्वष्टा न म इन्द्रश्च मे ॥ मरुतश्च म इन्द्रश्च मे ॥ विश्वे च मे देवा इन्द्रश्च मे ॥ यज्ञेन कल्पन्ताम् ॥

mitraśca ma indraśca me || varuṇaśca ma indraśca me || dhātā ca ma indraśca me || tvaṣṭā na ma indraśca me || marutaśca ma indraśca me || viśve ca me devā indraśca me || yajñena kalpantāṃ ||

And Friendship is within me, and the Rule of the Pure is within me, and Constancy is within me, and the Rule of the Pure is within me, and Creative Capacity is within me, and the Rule of the Pure is within me, and Skillful Design is within me, and the Rule of the Pure is within me, and Renunciation is within me, and the Rule of the Pure is within me, and all Gods of the Universe are within me, and the Rule of the Pure is within me, by means of sacrifice I conceive that all is within me.

- 18 -

पृथिवी च म इन्द्रश्च मे ॥ ऽन्तरिक्षं च म इन्द्रश्च मे ॥ द्यौश्च म इन्द्रश्च मे ॥ समाश्च म इन्द्रश्च मे ॥ नक्षत्राणि च म इन्द्रश्च मे ॥ दिशश्च म इन्द्रश्च मे ॥ यज्ञेन कल्पन्ताम् ॥

pṛthivī ca ma indraśca me || -ntarikṣaṃ ca ma indraśca me || dyauśca ma indraśca me || samāśca ma indraśca me || nakṣtrāṇi ca ma indraśca me || diśaśca ma indraśca me || yajñena kalpantāṃ ||

Earth is within me, and the Rule of the Pure is within me, and the atmosphere is within me, and the Rule of the Pure is within me, and heaven is within me, and the Rule of the Pure is within me, and All is within me, and the Rule of the Pure is within me, and the stars are within me, and the Rule of the Pure is within me, and all directions are within me, and the Rule of the Pure is within me, by means of sacrifice I conceive that all is within me.

- 19 -

अंशुश्च मे रश्मिश्च मे ॥ ऽदाभ्यश्च मेऽधिपतिश्च म ॥ उपांशुश्च मेऽन्तर्यामश्च म ॥ ऐन्द्रवायवश्च मे मैत्रावरुणश्च म ॥ आश्विनश्च मे प्रतिप्रस्थानश्च मे ॥ शुक्रश्च मे मन्थीच मे ॥ यज्ञेन कल्पन्ताम् ॥

aṃśuśca me raśmiśca me ll -dābhyaśca me-dhipatiśca ma ll upāṃśuśca me-rntāmaśca ma ll aindravāyavaśca me maitrāvaruṇaśca ma ll āśvinaśca me pratiprasthānaśca me ll śukraśca me manthīca me ll yajñena kalpantāṃ ll

Brilliant rays of light are within me, and beams of light are within me, and trustworthiness is within me, and the Lord is within me, and silent prayer is within me, and self-control is within me, and the Rule of Emancipated Spirit is within me, and the love of the Constant Flow is within me, and the Desire for Truth is within me, and every movement is within me, and radiance is within me, and the Nectar of Devotion is within me, by means of sacrifice I conceive that all is within me.

- 20 -

आग्रयणश्च मे वैश्वदेवश्च मे ॥ ध्रुवश्च मे वैश्वानरश्च म ॥ ऐन्द्राग्नश्च मे महावैश्वदेवश्च मे ॥ मरुत्वतीयाश्च मे निष्केवल्यश्च मे ॥ सावित्रश्च मे सारस्वतश्च मे ॥ पात्नीवतश्च मे हारियोजनश्च मे ॥ यज्ञेन कल्पन्ताम् ॥

āgrayaṇaśca me vaiśvadevaśca me ll dhruvaśca me vaiśvānaraśca ma ll aindrāgnaśca me mahāvaiśvadevaśca me ll marutvatīyāśca me niṣkevalyaśca me ll sāvitraśca me sārasvataśca me ll pātnīvataśca me hāriyojanaśca me ll yajñena kalpantāṃ ll

The time of sacrifice is within me, and all that is divine in the universe is within me, and the unchangeable is within me, and the divine light is within me, and the ruling blaze of purity is within me, and all the Gods in the universe are within me, and the joy of renunciation is within me, and non-attachment is within me, and the warmth of love is within me, and the essence of all is within me, and the joy of the Supreme is within me, and the fullness of unity is within me, by means of sacrifice I conceive that all is within me.

- 21 -

स्रुचश्च मे चमसाश्च मे ॥ वायव्यानि च मे द्रोणकलशश्च मे ॥ ग्रावणश्च मेऽधिषवणे च मे ॥ पुतभृच्च म आधवनीयश्च मे ॥ वेदिश्च मे बर्हिश्च मे ॥ ऽवभृथश्च मे स्वगाकारश्च मे ॥ यज्ञेन कल्पन्ताम् ॥

srucaśca me camasāśca me || vāyavyāni ca me droṇakalaśaśca me || grāvaṇaśca me-dhiṣavaṇe ca me || putabhṛcca ma ādhivanīyaśca me || vediśca me barhiśca me || -vabhṛthaśca me svagākāraśca me || yajñena kalpantāṃ ||

The sacrificial ladle is within me, and the vessels are within me, and the vessels of air are within me, and the vessels of water are within me, and the pressing stones are within me, and the strainer is within me, and the purified utensils are within me, and the utensils for stirring and cleaning are within me, and the purifying bathing of the sacrificer and cleansing of the vessels is within me, and the exclamations of mantras of offering are within me, by means of sacrifice I conceive that all is within me.

\- 22 -

अग्निश्च मे घर्मश्च मे ॥ ऽर्कश्च मे सूर्यश्च मे ॥ प्राणश्च मेऽश्वमे ॥ धश्च मे पृथिवी च मे ॥ ऽदितिश्च मे दितिश्च मे ॥ द्यौश्च मेऽङ्गलयः शक्करयो दिशश्च मे ॥ यज्ञेन कल्पन्ताम् ॥

agniśca me gharmaśca me ll -rkaśca me sūryaśca me ll prāṇaśca me -śvame ll dhaśca me pṛthivī ca me ll -ditiśca me ditiśca me ll dyauśca me -ṅgalayaḥ śakkarayo diśaśca me ll yajñena kalpantāṃ ll

The Divine Fire is within me, and heat is within me, and rays of light are within me, and the Light of Wisdom is within me, and Life is within me, and the sacrifice of the King of Kings is within me, and the earth is within me, and the Mother of Enlightenment is within me, and the conceptual world is within me, and heaven is within me, and powerful fingers in all directions are within me, by means of sacrifice I conceive that all is within me.

\- 23 -

व्रतं च म ऋतवश्च मे ॥ तपश्च मे संवत्सरश्च मे ॥ ऽहोरात्रे ऊर्वष्ठीवे बृहद्रथन्तरे च मे ॥ यज्ञेन कल्पन्ताम् ॥

vrataṃ ca ma ṛtavaśca me ll tapaśca me saṃvatsaraśca me ll -horātre ūrvaṣṭīve bṛhadrathantare ca me ll yajñena kalpantāṃ ll

Vows are within me, and honesty is within me, and the performance of disciplined austerity is within me, and the years are within me, and the great hymns of praise within me are as equally extensive as the vastness of the night, by means of sacrifice I conceive that all is within me.

- 24 -

एका च मे ॥ तिस्रश्च मे ॥ तिस्रश्च मे ॥ पञ्च च मे ॥ पञ्च च मे ॥ सप्त च मे ॥ सप्त च मे ॥ नव च मे ॥ नव च म ॥ एकादश च म ॥ एकादश च मे ॥ त्रयोदश च मे ॥ त्रयोदश च मे ॥ पञ्चदश च मे ॥ पञ्चदश च मे ॥ सप्तदश च मे ॥ सप्तदश च मे ॥ नवदश च मे ॥ नवदश च म ॥ एकविंशतिश्च म ॥ एकविंशतिश्च मे ॥ त्रयोविंशतिश्च मे ॥ त्रयोविंशतिश्च मे ॥ पञ्चविंशतिश्च मे ॥ पञ्चविंशतिश्च मे ॥ सप्तविंशतिश्च मे ॥ सप्तविंशतिश्च मे ॥ नवविंशतिश्च मे ॥ नवविंशतिश्च म ॥ एकत्रिंशच्च म ॥ एकत्रिंशच्च मे ॥ त्रयस्त्रिंशच्च मे ॥ यज्ञेन कल्पन्ताम् ॥

ekā ca me || tisraśca me || tisraśca me || pañca ca me || pañca ca me || sapta ca me || sapta ca me || nava ca me || nava ca ma || ekādaśa ca ma || ekādaśa ca me || trayodaśa ca me || trayodaśa ca me || pañcadaśa ca me || pañcadaśa ca me || saptadaśa ca me || saptadaśa ca me || navadaśa ca me || navadaśa ca ma || ekaviṃ śatiśca ma || ekaviṃ śatiśca me || trayoviṃ śatiśca me || trayoviṃ śatiśca me || pañcaviṃ śatiśca me || pañcaviṃ śatiśca me || saptaviṃ śatiśca me || saptaviṃ śatiśca me || navaviṃ śatiśca me || navaviṃ śatiśca ma || ekatriṃ śacca ma || ekatriṃ śacca me || trayastriṃ śacca me || yajñena kalpantāṃ ||

And one is within me, and three is within me, and three is within me, and five is within me, and five is within me, and seven is within me, and seven is within me, and nine is within me, and nine is within me, and eleven is within me, and eleven is within me, and thirteen is within me, and thirteen is within me, and fifteen is within me, and fifteen is within me, and seventeen is within me, and seventeen is within me, and nineteen is within me, and nineteen is within me, and twenty-one is within me, and twenty-one is within me, and twenty-three is within me, and twenty-three is within me, and twenty-five is within me, and twenty-five is within me, and twenty-seven is within me, and twenty-seven is within me, and twenty-nine is within me, and twenty-nine is within me, and thirty-one is within me, and thirty-one is within me, and thirty-three is within me, by means of sacrifice I conceive that all is within me.

- 25 -

चतस्रश्च मे ॥ ऽष्टौ च मे ॥ ऽष्टौ च मे ॥ द्वादश च मे ॥ द्वादश च मे ॥ षोडश च मे ॥ षोडश च मे ॥ विंशतिश्च मे ॥ विंशतिश्च मे ॥ चतुर्विंशतिश्च मे ॥ चतुर्विंशतिश्च मे ॥ ऽष्टाविंशतिश्च मे ॥ ऽष्टाविंशतिश्च मे ॥ द्वात्रिंशच्च मे ॥ द्वात्रिंशच्च मे ॥ षट्त्रिंशच्च मे ॥ षट्त्रिंशच्च मे ॥ चत्वारिंशच्च मे ॥ चत्वारिंशच्च मे ॥ चतुश्चत्वारिंशच्च मे ॥ चतुश्चत्वारिंशच्च मे ॥ ऽष्टाचत्वारिंशच्च मे ॥ यज्ञेन कल्पन्ताम् ॥

catasraśca me ll -ṣṭau ca me ll -ṣṭau ca me ll dvādaśa ca me ll dvādaśa ca me ll ṣoḍaśa ca me ll ṣoḍaśa ca me ll viṃ śatiśca me ll viṃ śatiśca me ll caturviṃ śatiśca me ll caturviṃ śatiśca me ll -ṣṭāviṃ śatiśca me ll -ṣṭāviṃ śatiśca me ll dvātriṃ śacca me ll dvātriṃ śacca me ll ṣaṭtriṃ śacca me ll ṣaṭtriṃ śacca me ll catvāriṃ śacca me ll catvāriṃ śacca me ll catuścatvāriṃ śacca me ll catuścatvāriṃ śacca me ll -ṣṭācatvāriṃ śacca me ll yajñena kalpantāṃ ll

And four is within me, and eight is within me, and eight is within me, and twelve is within me, and twelve is within me, and sixteen is within me, and sixteen is within me, and twenty is within me, and twenty is within me, and twenty-four is within me, and twenty-four is within me, and twenty-eight is within me, and twenty-eight is within me, and thirty-two is within me, and thirty-two is within me, and thirty-six is within me, and thirty-six is within me, and forty is within me, and forty is within me, and forty-four is within me, and forty-four is within me, and forty-eight is within me, by means of sacrifice I conceive that all is within me.

- 26 -

त्र्यविश्च मे त्र्यवी मे ॥ दित्यवाट् च मे दित्यौही च मे ॥
पञ्चाविश्च मे पञ्चावी च मे ॥ त्रिवत्सश्च मे त्रिवत्सा च मे ॥
तुर्यवाट् च मे तुर्यौही च मे ॥ यज्ञेन कल्पन्ताम् ॥

tryaviśca me tryavī me || dityavāṭ ca me dityauhī ca me || pañcāviśca me pañcāvī ca me || trivatsaśaca me trivatsā ca me || turyavāṭ ca me turyauhī ca me || yajñena kalpantām ||

Three sacrifices are within me, and three which convey are within me, and many mantras for offering oblations are within me, and many ideas for meditation are within me, and development to auspicious perfection is within me, and having entered perfection is within me, and beloved sons are within me, and three beloved daughters are within me, and the mantra used for offering the oblation of ultimate unity is within me, and the meditation of ultimate unity is within me, by means of sacrifice I conceive that all is within me.

- 27 -

पष्ठवाट् च मे पष्ठौही च म ॥ उक्षाच मे वशा च म ॥
ऋषभश्च मे वेहच्च मे ॥ ऽनड्वाँश्च मे धेनुश्च मे ॥ यज्ञेन
कल्पन्ताम् ॥

paṣṭavāṭ ca me paṣṭauhī ca ma ‖ ukṣāca me vaśā ca ma ‖ ṛṣabhaśca me vehacca me ‖ -naḍvāṁśca me dhenuśca me ‖ yajñena kalpantāṃ ‖

And the mantras used for the oblations of great respect are within me, and meditations of great respect are within me, and controlling the Power of Submission is within me, and the best and the most excellent is within me, and the endeavor is within me, and the strength of Emancipation is within me, and the gift of Illumination is within me, by means of sacrifice I conceive that all is within me.

- 28 -

वाजाय स्वाहा प्रसवाय स्वाहाऽपिजाय स्वाहा क्रतवे स्वाहा वसवे स्वाहाऽहर्पतये स्वाहाऽन्हेमुग्धाय स्वाहा मुग्धाय वैनंशिनाय स्वाहा विनंशिनऽआन्त्यायनाय स्वाहाऽऽन्त्याय भौवनाय स्वाहा भुवनस्य पतये स्वाहाऽधिपतये स्वाहा प्रजापतये स्वाहा ।

इयं ते राण्मित्राय यन्ताऽसि यमन ऊर्जे त्वा वृष्ट्यै त्वा प्रजानां त्वाऽऽधिपत्याय ॥

vājāya svāhā prasavāya svāhā-pijāya svāhā kratave svāhā vasave svāhā-harpataye svāhā-nhemugdhāya svāhā mugdhāya vainaṃ śināya svāhā vinaṃ śina-āntyāyanāya svāhā-ntyāya bhauvanāya svāhā bhuvanasya pataye svāhā-dhipataye svāhā prajāpataye svāhā

iyaṃ te rāṇimatrāya yantā-si yamana ūĵe tvā vṛṣṭyai tvā prajānāṃ tvā--dhipatyāya

To the Power, I am one with God! To the Delight of the Pursuit, I am one with God! To Rebirth, I am one with God! To Efficiency, I am one with God! To the treasure of Bliss, I am one with God! To the Lord of Day and Night, I am one with God! To the Days of Ignorance, I am one with God! To the Disappearance of Ignorance, I am one with God! To the Ones who finish their earthly concepts, I am one with God! To the Lord of Being, I am one with God! To the Supreme Lord, I am one with God! To the Lord of Creation, I am one with God!

We give our all to you, to our delighted Friend, You are the Guiding Controller of the Power of Life. You are the showering down of creation, you are all created beings, you are the Supreme Lord of All.

- 29 -

आयुर्यज्ञेन कल्पन्तां ॥ प्राणो यज्ञेन कल्पन्तां ॥ चक्षुर्यज्ञेन कल्पन्तां ॥ श्रोत्रं यज्ञेन कल्पन्तां ॥ वाग्यज्ञेन कल्पन्तां ॥ मनो यज्ञेन कल्पन्तां ॥ आत्मा यज्ञेन कल्पन्तां ॥ ब्रह्मा यज्ञेन कल्पन्तां ॥ ज्योतिर्यज्ञेन कल्पन्तां ॥ स्वर्यज्ञेन कल्पन्तां ॥ पृष्ठं यज्ञेन कल्पन्तां ॥ यज्ञो यज्ञेन कल्पन्ताम् ॥

स्तोमश्च यजुश्च ऋक् च साम च बृहच्च रथन्तरं च ।
स्वर्देवा अगन्मामृता अभूम प्रजापतेः प्रजा अभूम वेट् स्वाहा ॥

āyuryajñena kalpantāṃ || prāṇo yajñena kalpantāṃ || cakṣuryajñena kalpantāṃ || śrotraṃ yajñena kalpantāṃ || vāgyajñena kalpantāṃ || mano yajñena kalpantāṃ || ātmā yajñena kalpantāṃ || brahmā yajñena kalpantāṃ || jyotiryajñena kalpantāṃ || svaryajñena kalpantāṃ || pṛṣṭaṃ yajñena kalpantāṃ || yajño yajñena kalpantāṃ ||

stomaśca yajuśca ṛk ca sāma ca bṛhacca rathantaraṃ ca
svardevā aganmāmṛtā abhūma prajāpateḥ prajā abhūma veṭa svāhā

Humanity by means of sacrifice is contemplated; Life by means of sacrifice is contemplated; Sight by means of sacrifice is contemplated; Sound by means of sacrifice is contemplated; Vibrations by means of sacrifice are contemplated; Mind by means of sacrifice is contemplated; The Self by means of sacrifice is contemplated; The Supreme Creative Capacity by means of sacrifice is contemplated; The Light by means of sacrifice is contemplated; Heaven by means of sacrifice is contemplated; Rays of Light by means of sacrifice are contemplated; The sacrifice by means of sacrifice is contemplated. And the hymns of the Yajur Veda and the Ṛg Veda and the Sāma Veda are the great songs of praise to Wisdom. As Gods in heaven we have found the nectar of the Bliss of Immortality, and as the children of the Lord of Creation, we, ourselves, are immortal, I am one with God!

इति अष्टमोऽध्यायः

iti aṣṭamo-dhyāyaḥ

Thus ends the eighth chapter.

Chapter 9

हरिः ॐ

hariḥ oṃ

Praise to oṃ

\- 1 -

ऋचं वाचं प्र पद्ये मनो यजुः प्र पद्ये साम प्राणं प्र पद्ये
चक्षुः श्रोत्रं प्र पद्ये ।
वागोजः सहौजो मयि प्राणापानौ ॥

ṛcaṃ vācaṃ pra padye mano yajuḥ pra padye sāma prāṇaṃ pra padye cakṣuḥ śrotraṃ pra padye vāgojaḥ sahaujo mayi prāṇāpānau

May my voice be the expression of hymns. May my mind be filled with sacrifice. May my breath be the expression of divine songs. May my eyes and ears and other senses be filled with divine vibrations. May my inflowing breath be equal to my outflowing breath.

\- 2 -

यन्मे छिद्रं चक्षुषोत्हृदयस्य मनसो
वातितृण्णं बृहस्पतिर्मे तद्दधातु ।
शं नो भवतु भुवनस्यस्पतिः ॥

yanme chidraṃ cakṣuṣothṛdayasya manaso vātitṛṇṇaṃ bṛhaspatirme tad dadhātu śaṃ no bhavatu bhuvanasyaspatiḥ

Whatever deficiency fills my eyes, my heart, my mind, oh Guru of the Gods, Spirit of the Vast, please remove from me. May the Lord of the earth grant peace and bliss to us.

- 3 -

भूर्भुवः स्वः । तत् सवितुर्वरेण्यम् भर्गो देवस्य धीमहि ।

धियो यो नः प्रचोदयात् ॥

bhūr bhuvaḥ svaḥ tat savitur vareṇyam
bhargo devasya dhīmahi
dhiyo yo naḥ pracodayāt

The Infinite Beyond Conception, the gross body, the subtle body and the causal body; we meditate upon that Light of Wisdom which is the Supreme Wealth of the Gods. May it grant to us increase in our meditations.

- 4 -

कया नश्चित्र आ भुवदूती सदावृधः सखा ।

कया शचिष्ठया वृता ॥

kayā naścitra ā bhuvadūtī sadāvṛdhaḥ sakhā
kayā śaciṣṭayā vṛtā

With what spiritual discipline will the eternal definitely become our friend and help us?

- 5 -

कस्त्वा सत्यो मदानां मंहिष्ठो मत्सदन्धसः ।

दृढा चिदारुजे वसु ॥

kastvā satyo madānāṃ maṃhiṣto matsadandhasaḥ
dṛḍhā cidāruje vasu

Oh Lord, your truth is our food and is the true wealth to us. Fill our consciousness with consistency.

- 6 -

अभी षुणः सखीनामविता जरितॄणाम् ।

शतं भवास्यूतिभिः ॥

abhī ṣuṇo sakhīnāmavitā jaritṝṇām
śataṃ bhavāsyūtibhiḥ

Oh Lord, we sing your hymns and songs of divinity, protect us. With all your capacity protect us.

\- 7 -

कया त्वां न ऊत्याभि प्र मन्दसे वृषन् ।

कया स्तोतृभ्य आ भर ॥

kayā tvāṃ na ūtyābhi pra manadase vṛṣan
kayā stotṛbhya ā bhara

Oh Lord, which offerings fill you with delight? Which hymns and which songs bring you delight?

\- 8 -

इन्द्रो विश्वस्य राजति ।

शं नो अस्तु द्विपदे शं चतुपदे ॥

indro viśvasya rājati
śaṃ no astu dvipade śaṃ catupade

Indra is the king of the universe. May he grant peace and bliss to all beings who have two feet and four feet.

\- 9 -

शं नो मित्रः सं वरुणाः शं नो भवत्वर्यमा ।

शं न इन्द्रो बृहस्पतिः शं नो विष्णुरुरुक्रमः ॥

śaṃ no mitraḥ saṃ varuṇāḥ śaṃ no bhavatvaryamā
śaṃ na indro bṛhaspati śaṃ no viṣṇururukramaḥ

May Friendship grant us peace and bliss, may the Lord of Equilibrium grant us peace and bliss. May those purified by knowledge in the world give us peace and bliss. May the Rule of the Pure grant us peace and bliss, may the Lord of the Vast grant us peace and bliss. May the Lord Viṣṇu who pervades the universe grant us peace and bliss.

\- 10 -

शं नो वातः पवतां शं नस्तपतु सूर्यः ।

शं नः शनिक्रदद्देवः पर्जन्यो अभि वर्षतु ॥

śaṃ no vātaḥ pavatāṃ śaṃ nastapatu sūryaḥ
śaṃ no śanikradaḍevaḥ parjanyo abhi varṣatuḥ

May the Lord of Emancipation grant us peace and bliss through the wind. May the Sun, the Light of Wisdom, grant us peace and bliss through his light. May the Lord of Thunder who roars in the heavens, grant us peace and bliss through the rains.

- 11 -

अहानि शं भवन्तु नः शं रात्रीः प्रति धीयताम् ।

शं न इन्द्राग्नी भवतामवेभिः शं न इन्द्रावरुणा रातहव्या ।

शं न इन्द्रापुशणा वाजसातौ

शमिन्द्रासोमा सुविताय शं योः ॥

ahāni śaṃ bhavantu naḥ śaṃ rātrīḥ prati dhīyatām
śaṃ na indrāgnī bhavatāmavebhiḥ
śaṃ na indrāvaruṇā rātahavyā
śaṃ na indrāpuśaṇā vājasātau
śamindrāsomā suvitāya śaṃ yoḥ

May the Gods of the day grant us peace and bliss. May the Gods of the Night grant us peace and bliss. May Indra and Agni protect us and grant us peace and bliss. May Indra and Varuṇa, being delighted from our offerings, grant us peace and bliss. May Indra and Puṣa, in the form of nourishment, grant us peace and bliss. May Indra and Soma, in the form of devotion, destroying all disease and fear, grant us peace and bliss.

- 12 -

शं नो देवीरीभष्टय आपो भवन्तु पीतये ।

शं योरभि स्रवन्तु नः ॥

śaṃ no devīrībhaṣṭaya āpo bhavantu pītaye
śaṃ yorabhi sravantu naḥ

May all Goddesses grant us peace and bliss. May the waters that we drink grant us peace and bliss and save us from fear of disease.

- 13 -

स्योना पृथिवि नो भवानृक्षरा निवेशनी ।

यच्छा नः सर्म सप्रथाः ॥

syonā pṛthivi no bhavānṛkṣarā niveśanī
yacchā naḥ sarma saprathāḥ

Oh Earth, grant us delight. Give refuge to all.

- 14 -

आपो हिष्ठा मयोभुवस्ता न ऊर्जे दधातन ।

महे रणाय चक्षसे ॥

āpo hiṣṭhā mayobhuvastā na ūrje dadhātana
mahe raṇāya cakṣase

Oh Goddess of the Waters, you are the cause of all delight. Let us enjoy the nectar of bliss to the extent of our capacity. Empower us to receive the magnificent vision of the Supreme Divinity.

- 15 -

यो वः शिवतमो रसस्तस्य भाजयतेह नः ।

उशतीरिव मातरः ॥

yo vaḥ śivatamo rasastasya bhājayateha naḥ
uśatīriva mātaraḥ

Oh Divine Mother, just as you cause the infant children to drink nourishment from your breasts, just so, cause us to drink the nectar of delight.

- 16 -

तस्मा अरं गमाम वो यस्य क्षयाय जिन्वथ ।

आपो जनयथा च नः ॥

tasmā araṃ gamāma vo yasya kṣayāya jinvatha
āpo janayathā ca naḥ

Oh Divine Mother, you hold the nectar of infinite life. Again and again we come to receive these waters. Please grant them to us.

- 17 -

द्यौः शान्तिरन्तरिक्षं शान्तिः पृथिवी

शान्तिरापः शान्तिरोषधयः शान्तिः ।

वनस्पतयः शान्तिर्विश्वे देवाः शान्तिर्ब्रह्म शान्तिः सर्वꣳ

शान्तिः शान्तिरेव शान्तिः सा मा शान्तिरेधि ॥

dyauḥ śāntirantarikṣaṃ śāntaḥ pṛthivī śāntirāpaḥ
śāntiroṣadhayaḥ śāntiḥ
vanaspatayaḥ śāntirviśve devāḥ śāntirbrahma
śāntiḥ sarva guṃ śāntiḥ śāntireva śāntiḥ
sā mā śāntiredhiḥ

Peace in the heavens, Peace in the atmosphere, Peace on the earth, Peace to the waters, Peace to all vegetation, Peace to the spirit of all that lives. Peace to all Gods of the universe, Peace to Creative Consciousness, Peace to all. Peace, Peace, only Peace, equally Peace, by means of Peace.

- 18 -

दृते दृंह मा मित्रस्य मा चक्षुषा

सर्वाणि भूतानि समीक्षन्ताम् ।

मित्रस्याहं चक्षुषा सर्वाणि भूतानि समीक्षे ।

मित्रस्य चक्षुषा समीक्षामहे ॥

dṛte dṛṃha mā mitrasya mā cakṣuṣā
sarvāṇi bhūtāni samīkṣantām
mitrasyāhaṃ cakṣuṣā sarvāṇi bhūtāni samīkṣe
mitrasya cakṣuṣā samīkṣāmahe

Bless us with consistency. May all living beings see us through the eyes of Friendship. May we also see all living beings through the eyes of Friendship. May all beings see all existence through the eyes of Friendship.

- 19 -

दृते दृंहमा । ज्योक्ते सन्दृशि जीव्यासं

ज्योक्ते सन्दृशि जीव्यासम् ॥

dṛte dṛṃha mā jyokte sandṛśi jīvyāsaṃ
jyokte sandṛśi jīvyāsam

Bless us with consistency. Bless us with eternal life in the vision of you.

- 20 -

नमस्ते हरसे शोचिषे नमस्ते अस्त्वर्चिषे ।

अन्यांस्ते अस्मत्तपन्तु हेतयः पावको अस्मभ्यं शिवो भव ॥

namaste harase śociṣe namaste astvarciṣe
anyāṃste asmattapantu hetayaḥ
pāvako asmabhyaṃ śivo bhava

We bow to your illumination, Agni, Light of Purification. Purify us with your blazing illumination. Grant us purity and grant us peace.

- 21 -

नमस्ते अस्तु विद्युते नमस्ते स्तनयित्नवे ।

नमस्ते भगवन्नस्तु यतः स्वः समीहसे ॥

namaste astu vidyute namaste stanayitnave
namaste bhagavannastu yataḥ svaḥ samīhase

We bow to you, Supreme Divinity. We bow to you in the form of lightning. We bow to you in the form of thunder. Our endeavor is to show respect.

- 22 -

यतो यतः समीहसे ततो नो अभयं कुरु ।

शं नः कुरु प्रजाभ्योऽभयं नः पशुभ्यः ॥

yato yataḥ samīhase tato no abhayaṃ kuru
śaṃ naḥ kuru prajābhyo-bhayaṃ naḥ paśubhyaḥ

Wherever, whenever, we show respect, then and there you grant us freedom from fear. Give us peace and bliss, to all beings born, freedom from fear to us and to all animals, to all that lives.

- 23 -

सुमित्रिया न आप ओषधयः सन्तु
दुर्मित्रियास्तस्मै सन्तु योऽस्मान्
द्वेष्टि यंच वयं द्विष्मः ॥

sumitriyā na āpa oṣadhayaḥ santu
durmitriyāstasmai santu yo-smān
dveṣti yaṃca vayaṃ divaṣmaḥ

Let all waters and plants be friendly to us and to all our friends. May they not support any conflict or confusion.

- 24 -

तच्चक्षुर्देवहितं पुरस्ताच्छु क्रमुच्चरत् ॥ पश्येम शरदः ॥
शतं जीवेम शरदः ॥ शतं शृणुयाम शरदः ॥
शतं प्रब्रवाम शरदः ॥ शतमदीनाः स्याम शरदः ॥
शतं भूयश्चशरदः ॥ शतात् ॥ ॐ शान्तिः ॥

taccakṣurdevahitaṃ purastācchu kramuccarat || paśyema śaradaḥ || śataṃ jīvema śaradaḥ || śataṃ śṛṇuyāma śaradaḥ || śataṃ prabravāma śaradaḥ || śatamadīnāḥ syāma śaradaḥ || śataṃ bhūyaścaśaradaḥ || śatāt || oṃ śāntiḥ ||

May our eyes be for the benefit of the Gods, with purity like the eye of the rising sun on the eastern horizon. From that consecrated offering may we see for a hundred autumns. May our lives last a hundred autumns. May we hear for a hundred autumns. May we speak for a hundred autumns. May we maintain dependency on you for a hundred autumns. May we dwell with you for all eternity.

इति रुद्रपद्धतौशान्त्यिध्यायः

iti rudrapaddhatauśāntyadhyāyaḥ

Thus ends the peace chapter of the system of worship for Rudra.

हरिः ॐ

hariḥ oṃ

Praise to oṃ

ॐ सद्योजातं प्रपद्यामि सद्योजातायवै नमो नमः ।

भवे भवे नाति भवे भवस्वमांभवोद्भवाय नमः ॥

oṃ sadyojātaṃ prapadyāmi
sadyojātāyavai namo namaḥ
bhave bhave nāti bhave
bhavasvamāṃ bhavodbhavāya namaḥ

oṃ I extol the Birth of Truth as Pure Existence. Again and again I bow down to the Birth of Truth as Pure Existence. In being after being, beyond all being, who Himself is all Being, from whom came all being, to That Existence I bow.

वामदेवाय नमो ज्येष्ठाय नमः श्रेष्ठाय नमो रुद्राय नमः ।

कालाय नमः कलविकरणाय नमो बलविकरणाय नमो

बलाय नमो बलप्रमत्तनाय नमः । सर्वभूतदमनाय

नमोमनोन्मनाय नमः ॥

vāmadevāya namo jyeṣṭhāya namaḥ śreṣṭhāya
namo rudrāya namaḥ kālāya namaḥ
kalavikaraṇāya namo balavikaraṇāya namo
balāya namo balapramattanāya namaḥ
sarvabhūtadamanāya namomanonmanāya namaḥ

I bow to the Beautiful God who is Beloved. I bow to the Pleasant One, to the Ultimate One; I bow to the Reliever of Sufferings. I bow to Time, I bow to the Cause of the Illumination of Darkness, I bow to the Source of Strength, I bow to the Progenitor of Strength. I bow to the Fashioner of all the elements, I bow to the Mind of all minds.

अघोरेभ्योत्तघोरेभ्योघोरघेरतरेभ्यः ।

सर्वेभ्यःसर्वशर्वेभ्यो नमस्तेऽस्तुरुद्ररूपेभ्यः ॥

aghorebhyottaghorebhyoghoragheratarebhyaḥ sarvebhyaḥsarvaśarvebhyo namaste-sturudrarūpebhyaḥ

I bow to He who is Free From Fear, who instills the fear of evil, who saves the righteous from fear; who is within all, the all of everything, may we give our respect to He who is the form of the Reliever of Sufferings.

ॐ तत् पुरुषाय विद्महे महादेवाय धीमहि ।

तन्नो रुद्रः प्रचोदयात् ॥

oṃ tat puruṣāya vidmahe mahādevāya dhīmahi tanno rudraḥ pracodayāt

We meditate upon That Universal Consciousness, contemplate the Great God. May that Reliever of Sufferings grant us increase.

ईशानः सर्वविद्यानमीश्वरः सर्वभूतानाम् ।

ब्रह्माधिपतिर्ब्रह्मणोधिपतिर्ब्रह्माशिवोमेऽस्तुसदाशिवोम् ॥

īśānaḥ sarvavidyānamīśvaraḥ sarvabhūtānām brahmādhipatirbrahmaṇodhipatirbrahmāśivome-stusadāśivom

The Seer of All, who is all Knowledge, the Lord of the Universe, who is all existence; before the Creative Consciousness, before the knowers of Consciousness, existing in eternal delight as the Consciousness of Infinite Goodness.

kara nyāsa
establishment in the hands

ॐ नं अंगुष्ठाभ्यां नमः

oṃ naṃ aṅguṣṭhābhyāṃ namaḥ thumb forefinger
oṃ naṃ in the thumb I bow.

ॐ मः तर्जनीभ्यां स्वाहा

oṃ maḥ tarjanībhyāṃ svāhā thumb forefinger
oṃ maḥ in the forefinger, I am One with God!

ॐ शिं मध्यमाभ्यां वषट्

oṃ śiṃ madhyamābhyāṃ vaṣaṭ thumb middle finger
oṃ śiṃ in the middle finger, Purify!

ॐ वां अनामिकाभ्यां हुं

oṃ vāṃ anāmikābhyāṃ huṃ thumb ring finger
oṃ vāṃ in the ring finger, Cut the Ego!

ॐ यः कनिष्ठिकाभ्यां वौषट्

oṃ yaḥ kaniṣṭhikābhyāṃ vauṣaṭ thumb little finger
oṃ yaḥ in the little finger, Ultimate Purity!

Roll hand over hand forwards while reciting karatala kara and backwards while chanting pṛṣṭhābhyāṃ, then clap hands when chanting astrāya phaṭ.

ॐ नमः शिवाय करतल कर पृष्ठाभ्यां अस्त्राय फट् ॥

oṃ namaḥ śivāya karatala kara pṛṣṭhābhyāṃ astrāya phaṭ
oṃ I bow to the Consciousness of Infinite Goodness with the weapon of Virtue.

ॐ नमः शिवाय

oṃ namaḥ śivāya
oṃ I bow to the Consciousness of Infinite Goodness.

aṅga nyāsa
establishment in the body

Holding tattva mudrā, touch heart.

ॐ नं हृदयाय नमः

oṃ naṃ hṛdayāya namaḥ touch heart
oṃ naṃ in the heart, I bow.

Holding tattva mudrā touch top of head.

ॐ मः शिरसे स्वाहा

oṃ maḥ śirase svāhā top of head
oṃ maḥ on the top of the head, I am One with God!

With thumb extended, touch back of head.

ॐ शिं शिखायै वषट्

oṃ śiṃ śikhāyai vaṣaṭ back of head
oṃ śiṃ on the back of the head, Purify!

Holding tattva mudrā, cross both arms.

ॐ वां कवचाय हुं

oṃ vāṃ kavacāya huṃ cross both arms
oṃ vāṃ crossing both arms, Cut the Ego!

Holding tattva mudrā, touch three eyes at once with three middle fingers.

ॐ यः नेत्रत्रयाय वौषट्

oṃ yaḥ netratrayāya vauṣaṭ touch three eyes
oṃ yaḥ in the three eyes, Ultimate Purity!

Roll hand over hand forwards while reciting karatala kara and backwards while chanting pṛṣṭhābhyāṃ, then clap hands when chanting astrāya phaṭ.

ॐ नमः शिवाय करतल कर पृष्ठाभ्यां अस्त्राय फट् ॥

oṃ namaḥ śivāya karatala kara pṛṣṭhābhyāṃ astrāya phaṭ

oṃ I bow to the Consciousness of Infinite Goodness with the weapon of Virtue.

ॐ नमः शिवाय

oṃ namaḥ śivāya

I bow to the Consciousness of Infinite Goodness.

(108 times)

आरति

ārati

Dance in Celebration

जय शिव ॐकार । (बोलो) जय शिव ॐकार ।

ब्रह्म विष्णु सदा शिव । अर्धाङ्गि धारा ॥

ॐ हर हर हर महादेव ॥

jaya śiva oṃkāra, (bolo) jaya śiva oṃkāra
brahma viṣṇu sadā śiva, ardhāṅgi dhārā
oṃ hara hara hara mahādeva

Victory to Śiva, the Consciousness of Infinite Goodness, in the form of oṃ. Let's say, Victory to Śiva, the Consciousness of Infinite Goodness, in the form of oṃ. Creative Consciousness, Preserving Consciousness, and always the Consciousness of Continuous Transformation (as well as the Consciousness of Infinite Goodness) who with only His part supports all living beings. oṃ He Who Takes Away, He Who Takes Away, He Who Takes Away, the Great God.

एकानन चरानन पञ्चानन राजे, (शिव) पञ्चानन राजे ।

हंसासन गरुडासन । वृष वाहन ते सोहे ॥

ॐ हर हर हर महादेव ॥

ekā nana carā nana pañcā nana rāje,
(śiva) pañcā nana rāje haṃs āsana garuḍāsana
vṛṣa vāhana te sohe
oṃ hara hara hara mahādeva

He shows Himself with one face, with four faces and with five faces as well, Oh Śiva, with five faces as well. Sitting upon a swan, sitting upon the King of Birds, a golden eagle, sitting upon a bull. oṃ He Who Takes Away, He Who Takes Away, He Who Takes Away, the Great God.

दोय भूज च चतुर्भूज दशभूज ते सोहे,

(शिव) दशभूज ते सोहे ।

तीन रूप निराखता । त्रिभुवन जन मोहे ॥

ॐ हर हर हर महादेव ॥

doya bhūja ca caturbhūja daśabhūja te sohe,
(śiva) daśabhūja te sohe
tīna rūpa nirākhatā, tri bhuvana jana mohe
oṃ hara hara hara mahādeva

With two arms and with four arms and with ten arms as well, Oh Śiva, with ten arms as well. These three forms revolve, these three forms revolve in the ignorance of the inhabitants of the three worlds. oṃ He Who Takes Away, He Who Takes Away, He Who Takes Away, the Great God.

अक्षर्माला वनमाला रुण्डमाला धारि,

(शिव) रुण्डमाला धारि । चन्दन मृग मद चन्द ।

भले शुभकारी ॥ ॐ हर हर हर महादेव ॥

ākṣarmālā vanamālā ruṇḍamālā dhāri,
(śiva) ruṇḍamālā dhāri candana mṛga mada canda,
bhale śubha kārī
oṃ hara hara hara mahādeva

With a garland of letters, with a garland of forest flowers, with a garland of skulls as well, Oh Śiva, with a garland of skulls as well. With the scent of sandle, with the scent of musk, with the scent of spiritous liquor as well, truly you are the cause of purification. oṃ He Who Takes Away, He Who Takes Away, He Who Takes Away, the Great God.

श्वेताम्बर पिताम्बर बाघम्बर अङ्गे,

(शिव) बाघम्बर अङ्गे ।

सेनतादिक प्रभु तादिक । भूतादिक ते सङ्गे ॥

ॐ हर हर हर महादेव ॥

śvetāmbara pitāmbara bāghambara aṅge,
(śiva) bāghambara aṅge
senatādika prabhu tādika, bhūtādika te saṅge
oṃ hara hara hara mahādeva

With a white colored cloth, with a yellow colored cloth, with a tiger skin aparell as well, Oh Śiva, with a tiger skin apparell as well. With an army, as Lord of the armies, with an army, as Lord of the armies, and accompanied by an army of ghosts and goblins as well. oṃ He Who Takes Away, He Who Takes Away, He Who Takes Away, the Great God.

कर मध्ये कमण्डलु चक्र त्रिशूल धरता

(शिव) चक्र त्रिशूल धरता । जगत कर्ता जगत हर्ता ।

जगत पालन कर्ता ॥ ॐ हर हर हर महादेव ॥

kara madhye kamaṇḍalu cakra triśūla dharatā,
(śiva) cakra triśūla dharatā, jagata kartā jagata hartā
jagata pālana kartā, oṃ hara hara hara mahādeva

In His hands He holds a water pot, a discus, and a trident as well, Oh Śiva, a discus and a trident as well. He makes the perceivable universe, and He takes away the perceivable universe, and He protects the perceivable universe as well. oṃ He Who Takes Away, He Who Takes Away, He Who Takes Away, the Great God.

ब्रह्म विष्णु सदाशिव जनत आविवेका,

(शिव) जनत आविवेका ।

प्रनव आक्षर ॐमध्ये । ये तीनो एका ॥

ॐ हर हर हर महादेव ॥

brahma viṣṇu sadāśiva janata āvivekā, (śiva) janata āvivekā pranava ākṣara oṃ madhye, ye tīna ekā oṃ hara hara hara mahādeva

Creative Conciousness, Preserving Consciousness, and always the Consciousness of Continuous Transformation (as well as the Consciousness of Infinite Goodness), to those people without discrimination (appear separate). But within the holy syllable oṃ, but within the holy syllable oṃ, the three are actually ONE. oṃ He Who Takes Away, He Who Takes Away, He Who Takes Away, the Great God.

त्रिगुण स्वामि कि आरति यो कोइ नर गावे,

(शिव) यो कोइ नर गावे । बनात शिवानन्द स्वामि ।

वञ्चित फल पह्वे ॥ ॐ हर हर हर महादेव ॥

triguṇa svāmi ki ārati yo koi nara gāve, (śiva) yo koi nara gāve, banāta śivānanda svāmi vañcita phala pahve, oṃ hara hara hara mahādeva

Whatever man will sing this praise of the Master of the three gunas (qualities), Oh Śiva, whatever man will sing. Make him a master of the Bliss of Infinite Consciousness, make him a master of the Bliss of Infinite Consciousness, certainly that will be the fruit he receives. oṃ He Who Takes Away, He Who Takes Away, He Who Takes Away, the Great God.

जय शिव ॐकार । (बोलो) जय शिव ॐकार ।
ब्रह्म विष्णु सदा शिव । अर्धाङ्गि धारा ॥
ॐ हर हर हर महादेव ॥

jaya śiva oṃkāra, (bolo) jaya śiva oṃkāra
brahma viṣṇu sadā śiva, ardhāṅgi dhārā
oṃ hara hara hara mahādeva

Victory to Śiva, the Consciousness of Infinite Goodness, in the form of oṃ. Let's say, Victory to Śiva, the Consciousness of Infinite Goodness, in the form of oṃ. Creative Consciousness, Preserving Consciousness, and always the Consciousness of Continuous Transformation (as well as the Consciousness of Infinite Goodness) who with only His part supports all living beings. oṃ He Who Takes Away, He Who Takes Away, He Who Takes Away, the Great God.

प्रणाम्
praṇām

ॐ महादेव महात्राण महायोगि महेश्वर ।
सर्वपापहरां देव मकाराय नमो नमः ॥

oṃ mahādeva mahātrāṇa mahāyogi maheśvara
sarvapāpaharāṃ deva makārāya namo namaḥ

oṃ The Great God, the Great Reliever, the Great Yogi, Oh Supreme Lord, Oh God who removes all Sin, in the form of the letter "M" which dissolves creation, we bow to you again and again.

ॐ नमः शिवाय शान्ताय कारणत्रय हेतवे ।
निवेदयामि चात्मानं त्वं गतिः परमेश्वर ॥

oṃ namaḥ śivāya śāntāya kāraṇatraya hetave
nivedayāmi cātmānaṃ tvaṃ gatiḥ parameśvara

oṃ I bow to the Consciousness of Infinite Goodness, to Peace, to the Cause of the three worlds, I offer to you the fullness of my soul, Oh Supreme Lord.

त्वमेव माता च पिता त्वमेव त्वमेव बन्धुश्च सखा त्वमेव ।
त्वमेव विद्या द्रविणं त्वमेव त्वमेव सर्वम् मम देवदेव ॥

tvameva mātā ca pitā tvameva
tvameva bandhuśca sakhā tvameva
tvameva vidyā draviṇaṃ tvameva
tvameva sarvam mama deva deva

You alone are Mother and Father, you alone are friend and relative. You alone are knowledge and wealth, Oh my God of Gods, you alone are everything.

कायेन वाचा मनसेन्द्रियैर्वा बुद्ध्यात्मानवप्रकृतस्वभावत् ।
करोमि यद्यत् सकलम् परस्मै नारायणायेति समर्पयामि ॥

kāyena vācā manasendriyairvā
buddhyātmā nava prakṛta svabhavat
karomi yadyat sakalam parasmai
nārāyaṇāyeti samarpayāmi

Body, speech, mind, the five organs of knowledge (five senses) and the intellect; these nine are the natural condition of human existence. In their highest evolution, I move beyond them all, as I surrender completely to the Supreme Consciousness.

ॐ पापोऽहं पापकर्माहं पापात्मा पापसम्भव ।
त्राहि मां पुण्डरीकाक्षं सर्वपापहरो हरिः ॥

oṃ pāpo-haṃ pāpakarmāhaṃ
pāpātmā pāpasambhava
trāhi māṃ puṇḍarīkākṣaṃ sarvapāpa haro hariḥ

oṃ I am of sin, confusion, duality; my actions are of duality; this entire existence is of duality. Oh Savior and Protector, Oh Great Consciousness, take away all sin, confusion, duality.

ॐ मन्त्रहीनं क्रियाहीनं भक्तिहीनं सुरेश्वरि ।
यत्पूजितं मया देवि परिपूर्णं तदस्तु मे ॥

oṃ mantrahīnaṃ kriyāhīnaṃ
bhaktihīnaṃ sureśvari
yatpūjitaṃ mayā devi paripūrnaṃ tadastu me

oṃ I know nothing of mantras. I do not perform good conduct. I have no devotion, Oh Supreme Goddess. But Oh my God, please accept the worship that I offer.

त्वमेव प्रत्यक्षम् ब्रह्माऽसि ।

त्वामेव प्रत्यक्षम् ब्रह्म वदिष्यामि ।

ऋतम् वदिष्यामि सत्यम् वदिष्यामि ।

तन मामवतु तद वक्तारमवतु ।

अवतु माम् अवतु वक्तारम् ॥

tvameva pratyakṣam brahmā-si
tvāmeva pratyakṣam brahma vadiṣyāmi
ṛtam vadiṣyāmi satyam vadiṣyāmi
tana māmavatu tada vaktāramavatu
avatu mām avatu vaktāram

You alone are the Perceivable Supreme Divinity. You alone are the Perceivable Supreme Divinity, so I shall declare. I shall speak the nectar of immortality. I shall speak Truth. May this body be your instrument. May this mouth be your instrument. May the Divine always be with us. May it be thus.

ॐ सह नाववतु सह नौ भुनक्तु । सह वीर्यं करवावहै ।

तेजस्विनावधीतमस्तु । मा विद्विषावहै ॥

oṃ saha nāvavatu, saha nau bhunaktu
saha vīryam karavāvahai tejasvināvadhītamastu
mā vidviṣāvahai

oṃ May the Lord protect us. May the Lord grant us enjoyment of all actions. May we be granted strength to work together. May our studies be thorough and faithful. May all disagreement cease.

ॐ असतो मा सद् गमय । तमसो मा ज्योतिर्गमय ।

मृत्योर्मा अमृतं गमय ॥

oṃ asatomā sad gamaya tamasomā jyotirgamaya
mṛtyormā amṛtaṃ gamaya

oṃ From untruth lead us to Truth. From darkness lead us to the Light. From death lead us to Immortality.

ॐ सर्वेषां स्वस्तिर्भवतु । सर्वेषां शान्तिर्भवतु । सर्वेषां पूर्णं भवतु । सर्वेषां मङ्गलं भवतु सर्वे भवन्तु सुखिनः । सर्वे सन्तु निरामयाः । सर्वे भद्राणि पश्यन्तु । मा कश्चिद् दुःख भाग्भवेत् ॥

oṃ sarveṣāṃ svastir bhavatu sarveṣāṃ śāntir bhavatu sarveṣāṃ pūrṇaṃ bhavatu sarveṣaṃ maṅgalaṃ bhavatu sarve bhavantu sukhinaḥ sarve santu nirāmayāḥ sarve bhadrāṇi paśyantu mā kaścid duḥkha bhāgbhavet

oṃ May all be blessed with the highest realization. May all be blessed with Peace. May all be blessed with Perfection. May all be blessed with Welfare. May all be blessed with comfort and happiness. May all be free from misery. May all perceive auspiciousness. May all be free from infirmities.

गुरुर्ब्रह्मा गुरुर्विष्णुः गुरुर्देवो महेश्वरः ।
गुरुः साक्षात् परं ब्रह्म तस्मै श्रीगुरवे नमः ॥

gurur brahmā gururviṣṇuḥ gururdevo maheśvaraḥ guruḥ sākṣāt paraṃ brahma tasmai śrīgurave namaḥ

The Guru is Brahmā, Guru is Viṣṇu, Guru is the Lord Maheśvara. The Guru is actually the Supreme Divinity, and therefore we bow down to the Guru.

ॐ ब्रह्मार्पणं ब्रह्म हविर्ब्रह्माग्नौ ब्रह्मणा हुतम् ।
ब्रह्मैव तेन गन्तव्यं ब्रह्मकर्मसमाधिना ॥

oṃ brahmārpaṇaṃ brahma havir
brahmāgnau brahmaṇā hutam
brahmaiva tena gantavyaṃ
brahmakarma samādhinā

oṃ The Supreme Divinity makes the offering; the Supreme Divinity is the offering; offered by the Supreme Divinity, in the fire of the Supreme Divinity. By seeing the Supreme Divinity in all actions, one realizes that Supreme Divinity.

ॐ पूर्णमदः पूर्णमिदं पूर्णात् पूर्णमुदच्यते ।
पूर्णस्य पूर्णमादाय पूर्णमेवावशिष्यते ॥

oṃ pūrṇamadaḥ pūrṇamidaṃ
pūrṇāt pūrṇamudacyate
pūrṇasya pūrṇamādāya pūrṇamevāva śiṣyate

oṃ That is whole and perfect; this is whole and perfect. From the whole and perfect, the whole and perfect becomes manifest. If the whole and perfect issue forth from the whole and perfect, even still only the whole and perfect will remain.

ॐ शान्तिः शान्तिः शान्तिः

oṃ śāntiḥ śāntiḥ śāntiḥ

oṃ Peace, Peace, Peace

More Books by Shree Maa and Swami Satyananda Saraswati

Annapūrṇa Thousand Names
Before Becoming This
Bhagavad Gītā
Chaṇḍi Pāṭh
Cosmic Pūjā
Cosmic Pūjā Bengali
Devī Gītā
Devī Mandir Songbook
Durgā Pūjā Beginner
Ganeśa Pūjā
Gems From the Chaṇḍi
Guru Gītā
Hanumān Pūjā
Kālī Dhyānam
Kālī Pūjā
Lakṣmī Sahasra Nāma
Lalitā Triśati
Rudrāṣṭādhyāyī
Sahib Sadhu
Saraswati Pūjā for Children
Shree Maa's Favorite Recipes
Shree Maa - The Guru & the Goddess
Shree Maa, The Life of a Saint
Śiva Pūjā Beginner
Śiva Pūjā and Advanced Fire Ceremony
Sundara Kāṇḍa
Swāmī Purāṇa
Thousand Names of Ganeśa
Thousand Names of Gayatri
Thousand Names of Viṣṇu and
Satya Nārāyaṇa Vrata Kathā

CDs and Cassettes

Chaṇḍi Pāṭh
Durgā Pūjā Beginner
Lalitā Triśati
Mantras of the Nine Planets
Navarṇa Mantra
Oh Dark Night Mother
Oṃ Mantra
Sādhu Stories from the Himalayas
Shree Maa at the Devi Mandir
Shree Maa in the Temple of the Heart
Shiva is in My Heart
Shree Maa on Tour, 1998
Śiva Pūjā Beginner
Śiva Pūjā and Advanced Fire Ceremony
The Goddess is Everywhere
The Songs of Ramprasad
The Thousand Names of Kālī
Tryambakaṃ Mantra

Videos

Across the States with Shree Maa & Swamiji
Meaning and Method of Worship
Shree Maa: Meeting a Modern Saint
Visiting India with Shree Maa and Swamiji

Please visit us at www.shreemaa.org
Our email is info@shreemaa.org

Blessings!

Lightning Source UK Ltd.
Milton Keynes UK
UKHW012041130522
402983UK00001B/27

9 781877 795534